Awesome Snake Science!

40 Activities for
Learning About Snakes

Cindy Blobaum

CHICAGO REVIEW PRESS

Published by Chicago Review Press, Incorporated
814 North Franklin Street
Chicago, Illinois 60610
ISBN 978-1-56976-807-5

Library of Congress Cataloging-in-Publication Data
Blobaum, Cindy, 1966-
    Awesome snake science : 40 activities for learning about snakes / Cindy
Blobaum. — 1st ed.
        p. cm.
    Includes bibliographical references and index.
    ISBN 978-1-56976-807-5 (pbk.)
    1. Snakes—Juvenile literature. 2. Snakes—Experiments—Juvenile literature.
3. Snakes—Study and teaching (Elementary)—Activity programs. I. Title.

    QL666.O6B64 2012
    597.96071—dc23
                                                                2011050257

Snake Identification
Snakes come in a wide range of colors and sizes. Here are the snakes shown in
full color on the covers of this book.

Front Cover:
Top: Royal python
First column: Ribbon snake (top) and a king snake skeleton
Second column: Snakes eggs (top) and a corn snake.
Third column: Parrot snake
Fourth column: Red-sided garter snake

Back Cover:
Left to right: Sinaloan milk snake, western rattlesnake, eastern coral snake,
    and malaysian king cobra.

Cover design: Joan Sommers Design, Chicago
Front cover photographs (clockwise from top): Royal Python © Ian McDonnell / iStockphoto;
    Red-sided Garter snake © Sharon Werenich/www.chickadeephotoart.com; Parrot Snake
    © Andrew M. Snyder; snake eggs © Annda Purdue; corn snake © Christian Weibell/
    iStockphoto; skeleton courtesy DigiMorph; Ribbon snake © John J. Mosesso/life.nbii.gov.
Back cover photographs (left to right): Sinaloan Milk Snake © William Loy / iStockphoto;
    Western Rattlesnake © Steve Mcsweeny / iStockphoto; Eastern Coral Snake © Mark
    Kostich / iStockphoto; Malaysian King Cobra © Omar Ariff / iStockphoto
Interior design: Scott Rattray
Interior illustrations: Gail Rattray
Photo credits: All photographs courtesy of Cindy Blobaum unless otherwise noted. Spot art of
    snakes © iStockphoto

Printed in the United States of America
5 4 3 2 1

For Lee, who explores his interests
with great enthusiasm.

Contents

Acknowledgments

I have never known a book to be written and produced without the assistance and encouragement of many people, and this book is no exception. I am grateful to the staff of the Dallas County Conservation Board who ignited the spark for this book by encouraging me to design interactive components for a traveling snake exhibit, unearthing a long-dormant interest in teaching about these wonderful animals. Once I started, I relied on my children, their friends, and available neighbor kids to test activities and act as models. My husband, Phil, was always a willing photographer, and his organizational skills and diligence in downloading and labeling images saved me more than once. Many scientists, natural resource managers, naturalists, and photographers were quite helpful, and generous with their knowledge and their images. Their interest in the project kept me going. However, none of this would matter if it weren't for the support and assistance provided by the staff at Chicago Review Press. Thank you for your belief in this project.

Introduction

A number of years ago my uncle, John Torline, handed me a white, flat box. "You're the one person I know who would appreciate this," he said. "I found it in my cabin."

I opened the box, lifted a layer of cotton batting, and saw a partially decomposed, partially mummified snake. Some of the skeleton was visible, as was the snake's final meal—one mouse in the belly and one mouse just by its mouth. I was delighted.

This gift may seem quite unusual, but it was from an uncle who obviously understands and supports what I do. I'm not surprised by his support. When I was a child, I would tiptoe to his aquarium to peer at the live rattlesnakes he had captured. I don't

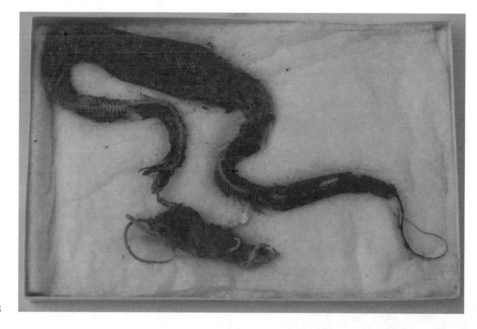

remember them being very active, but I could occasionally hear a soft buzz.

I didn't realize at the time how much this experience made an impression on me. My early exposure to snakes undoubtedly helped me to feel more comfort-

able around and interested in them. When I got my first real job as a seasonal keeper at a local zoo, I sometimes fed, watered, cleaned up after, and handled the snakes. I later worked in nature centers, where snakes are often kept as educational animals. Almost daily

I had a snake in my hand, encouraging people of all ages to touch it as they asked questions and learned more about the adaptations and ecological value of these fascinating creatures. I came up with The Secret of a Snake's Swallow project on page 24 to help a young girl understand how snake jaws work. The success of that demonstration inspired me to try to develop even more projects and activities.

Although you can learn and teach a lot when you have a snake in hand, the activities in this book are designed to help you learn more about snakes without needing to have a snake right in front of you. Do these projects to gain a good foundation of basic knowledge about snakes. To see what you learn come to life, visit nature centers, museums, and zoos to view live snakes. Then head outside to find, observe, and record what snakes you see in your area, keeping in mind that snakes are wild creatures that deserve respect and protection. Their numbers are dwindling in the wild, even as our interest in them and knowledge about them increases. So move one away from harm if necessary, but don't take it home and put in an aquarium.

If you want to work with live snakes, volunteer your time to help someone around you who already has snakes. Zoos, nature centers, science classrooms, pet stores, or animal rescue facilities are all places that might house snakes. The people in these places can teach you how to properly handle, care for, house, feed, and treat captive snakes. Experiences like these will be valuable if you decide to continue your study of snakes by joining snake scientists working with wild snakes in the field. There is a lot to learn about snakes, and the world needs more snake scientists. If you are ready to become one, flip the page and get started!

Snake Study

Look around—you are surrounded by snakes. Where are they? On flags and signs; on bodies as tattoos; as a part of the medical symbol in pharmacies and doctors' offices; in books, movies, and games; and on exhibit in pet stores, museums, nature centers, and zoos. Unless you are in a polar region, on top of very high mountains, or on the islands of Ireland, New Zealand, or Greenland, live snakes are outside and likely not too far away. There are around 3,000 different kinds of snakes living around the world,

DONT TREAD ON ME

www.Gadsden.info

omy (parts of the body) and the physiology (how the body systems work) of snakes. Scientists knew a lot about snakes but not much about what they needed to live and reproduce in the wild. Only recently have a growing number of scientists started concentrating their studies on the natural ecology and conservation of snakes.

During their studies, ophiologists (off-ee-all-uh-jists; snake scientists) came to a shocking realization. Just as they were starting to do more field studies about snakes, it was becoming harder to find snakes. Many species of snakes are in danger of becoming extinct.

There are many reasons snake populations are declining—their **habitats** are being destroyed, too many of them are captured for food and the pet trade, sometimes new animals that are introduced into snake habitats either hunt the snakes or eat their food, and snake

roundups (contests to find and kill as many snakes as possible) are just a few. If snakes were to disappear, there could be a huge increase in the populations of their **prey**—from insects to mice and even slugs! Scientists are concerned that most people don't understand how vital snakes are to the health of our environment. All these factors make it more important now than ever for people to learn all they can about snakes.

Snake Science

Many people know the word **herpetology,** but very few know the word **ophiology.** Herpetology is the study of all reptiles and amphibians, a large group of animals that includes turtles, lizards, snakes, tuataras, crocodiles, frogs, toads, salamanders, newts, and efts. Ophiology is the study of just one of those groups of animals—snakes.

including the sea snakes swimming in the warm waters of the Pacific and Indian oceans, the European adder living just above the Arctic Circle, and the common garter snakes and brown snakes that call many lawns, golf courses, and vacant lots home. Even more exciting, scientists believe there are snakes that have yet to be discovered!

Snakes are fascinating **reptiles** that have long been both feared and revered by humans. People

have hunted snakes, drawn snakes, written about snakes, built snake statues, and even created snake jewelry for millennia, with the oldest snake artwork being made well over 10,000 years ago. People eat snake meat, wear snake leather, keep snakes as pets, milk snakes for their **venom,** use snakes for religious ceremonies, visit snake museums, and line up to touch live snakes. Even with all this interest, for many years most snake studies focused on the **anat-**

Most scientists consider the Antiguan racer to be the rarest snake in the world. It is only found on Great Bird Island off the coast of Antigua, a small island in the Caribbean. Scientists rediscovered the snake in the early 1990s and have been working ever since to repair the snakes' habitat, remove the alien species, and help the snakes breed. In just 15 years, the population of the racer has gone from 50 to over 500!

The Blobaum family at Rattlesnake Bridge in Tucson, Arizona.

By reading the chapters and doing the activities, you will learn not only about the anatomy and physiology of snakes but also about projects around the world designed to save snakes. Armed with this information, you can become a snake ambassador, educating your family and friends about the wonders of snakes.

Make a Research Journal

Good scientists keep records of their observations, experiments, results, discoveries, questions, ideas, and even their conversations. Many of the activities in this book include making charts that will help you keep the information in order, which will make the data easier to understand. Sometimes an activity will make you think of other questions. Write down all these things in your research journal so you don't forget them.

Materials

3-ring binder with pockets
Pencils
10 dividers
Lined paper
Glue stick
Scissors

Label the dividers, and put 10 sheets of paper in each section:

Snake Sightings

Every time you see a snake or the image of a snake, record the date, what you saw, and where you saw it. Glue in photos you have taken, pictures, comics, and ads from magazines and newspapers. Be sure to add drawings of your own!

Experiments

This is where you record the results of your activities. Don't forget to write the name of each experiment at the top of the page.

Facts

In this section, write down any interesting information you see or hear about snakes.

Questions

It's easy to think of questions as you are doing something, and it's easy to forget your questions if you don't write them down. Leave a few lines after the question so you can write down the answer if you discover it later.

Resources

Write down the names and authors of books you read or the URLs of helpful websites. As you get to know snake scientists, record their names, mailing addresses, e-mail addresses, and phone numbers so you can contact them if you have questions or ideas.

Keep a few extra dividers available to make new sections as you need them. For example, if you volunteer at a nature center to help take care of snakes, keep track of your hours and experiences in a special section.

Use the pockets to hold a couple of pencils, a pair of scissors, a glue stick, a field guide, and the snake string you make in a later activity.

Seeing Snakes

Once you start looking for snakes, you start seeing more and more of them. **Researchers** have been studying people's ability to see snakes by using a touch-screen computer to measure reaction times. They asked people to look at a group of nine pictures that were shown on the screen at the same time and touch a certain one. All the participants, from age three through adult, found snake pictures faster than they found a picture of a flower, frog, or caterpillar.

Spot the Snakes

See how long it takes you to complete this test, and then time your family and friends doing the same test.

Materials

Stopwatch

Time how long it takes to follow the instructions at the top of the next two pages. Start the stopwatch as you turn this page, and stop it when you complete the task. Record your time, and then reset the stopwatch before you turn to the next page.

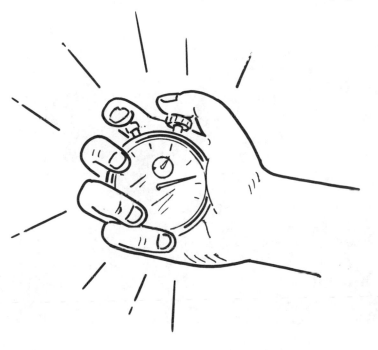

Touch the caterpillar picture.

John J. Mosesso/life.nbii.gov

David Cappaert, Michigan State University, Bugwood.org

US Fish and Wildlife Service

Pete Pattavina/US Fish and Wildlife Service

Touch the snake picture.

Gary M. Stolz/US Fish and Wildlife Service

Steve Bauer/www.ars.usda.gov

John J. Mosesso/life.nbii.gov

Ryan Haggerty/US Fish and Wildlife Service

Even though people react quickly to pictures of snakes and to wild snakes if they see them, most people walk right by a live snake in the outdoors and never see it. Even seasoned snake scientists admit to walking within inches of a snake without noticing it is there. If you do see a live snake and tell someone about it, one of the first things they'll ask is "How big was it?" If you were lucky, the snake was still and you got a good look at it. Most likely, you only saw a small portion of the snake for a very short time. But people will still want a guesstimate—a guessed estimate of both its length and weight.

Snakes come in many sizes; they can be long and thin, short and heavy, or any other combination. Size differences depend on the type and age of the snake, and how well it has eaten. A mature Prairie ringneck snake might be 14 inches (36 cm) long, the same length as a hatchling ball python, but you would never mistake one for the other. The adult ringneck snake would have about the same **diameter** as a pencil, while the young python's diameter would be closer to that of a thick marker. African egg-eating snakes, which can only find their food during a few months each year, can be quite skinny before birds start to nest each spring. They make up for it by gorging on eggs as long as they can, gaining a lot of weight before the end of the season. Of course, snakes are also individuals, even if they are of the same species. One nearly 6-foot (181-cm) long boa was recorded at 5.25 pounds (2.4 kg), while another nearly 6-foot (178-cm) long boa was only 2.25 pounds (1.03 kg).

How long is this snake?

Philip Blobaum

Snake String

Being able to accurately estimate lengths is a valuable skill for studying snakes and other animals, as the size of the animal is often a clue to its identity.

Materials

Ruler

Roll of wide, light-colored ribbon

Markers or labels, in several
    different colors

Use a ruler to mark inches or centimeters on one side of the ribbon. On the other side, use various colors of markers or sticky labels to mark the normal lengths of adult snakes often found in your area.*

Coil up the snake string and keep it in the pocket of your journal, ready to measure things you find.

Record Snake Sizes

Smallest	Thread snake	Under 4 inches (10 cm)
Longest	Reticulated python	33 feet (10 m)
Heaviest	Anaconda	Around 500 pounds (227 kg)
Largest fossil snake	Found in a coal mine in Columbia, South America in 2008.	Estimated to have been 43 feet long (13 m) and to have weighed 2,500 pounds (1134 kg)!

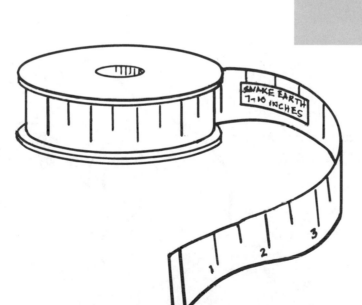

*Most states have online guides to local snakes. Type your state name and snakes (e.g., "Iowa snakes") into a search engine to find one for your area.

Snake Survey

Distance	Item	Position	Estimated length	Actual/measured length

How good are you at estimating the lengths of snakes? Use your snake string to take a survey of a yard full of fake snakes!

Materials

Friend

Fake snakes: 10 or more snake-shaped items, long and short, skinny and fat (yarn, rope, shoe-laces, belts, hoses, tubes, and, of course, toy snakes)

Notebook paper

Pencil

Snake string

Have a friend scatter the fake snakes outside, putting some into coils, partially hiding others, and if possible putting one in a body of water.

Make a chart on your paper like the one shown here.

Snake scientists rarely catch, hold, and measure every snake they see. For this activity, you can

- pick up three snakes;
- stand or kneel next to three snakes without touching them; and
- stay at least 10 steps away from four snakes.

When you first spot a snake, decide how close you can get to it and mark this distance in the first column on your chart. Then record the type of each snake in the second column (shoelace snake, spaghetti snake, etc.); whether its position was straight, coiled, half hidden, and so on in the third column; and your estimate of its length in the fourth column.

After you have estimated the length of each one, gather all the fake snakes and measure each one with the snake string. Write these numbers in the final column. Compare your estimates to the actual lengths. You can save your chart in your research journal.

Most people overestimate the length of snakes they see. One reason is that the bigger the snake, the better the story. Of course, there are other things that can affect your estimate. Based on your experience, would you believe an estimate made if someone saw

only part of a snake? A snake that was coiled? A snake that was far away? Is it easier to overestimate the length of thick-bodied snakes or thin ones? What happens when something is in water?

To improve your field estimating abilities, learn the lengths of

some common outdoor items. Measure the length of your hand and your foot, a section of sidewalk, a car tire, a stripe in the middle of a road, and the width of a lane in the road. Use these items as references and practice estimating the length of sticks, ropes,

leaves, and other things you see lying on the ground.

Explorers in South America from the 1700s up to the present day have told stories of seeing snakes that were 50 feet (15.2 m),

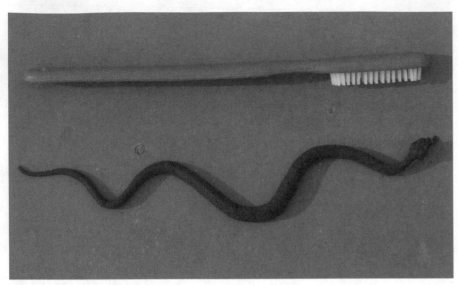

How long is this snake?

For smaller snakes, some scientists place the snake alongside a ruler and try to stretch it out. If a snake is too difficult to straighten out or too dangerous to handle, they put it in a squeeze box, which has foam cushioning on the sides and bottom and a clear plate on top. This keeps the snake from moving while the scientists lay a piece of string along its back to measure the snake. Some snakes, like anacondas, are too big for a squeeze box and might not want to hold still. So scientists use a flexible or cloth tape they lay on top of the snake.

Some people claim to have photographic proof of giant snakes. Type "giant rattlesnake" into an Internet search engine and you're sure to get lots of hits that will lead you to pictures of snakes that are supposed to be super long and really heavy. Take another look at the pictures on pages 8

90 feet (27.4 m), even 156 feet (47.5 m) long—that's over half the length of a football field! Of course, in most of these cases, no one actually measured the giant snakes, had pictures of them, or even brought back a skin, so scientists doubt the snakes were really that long.

When there are pictures, skins, or measurements, scientists often still doubt the reported size of giant snakes. You might think it would be easy to measure a snake you are holding, but live snakes rarely hold still in a straight line, their strong muscles make it almost impossible to straighten them out, and dead snakes or skins are easily stretched. Accurately measuring snakes, especially the big ones, has always been a challenge. There is also the question of what should be measured. Some scientists measure the total length, others measure from the tip of the nose to the start of the tail, and some record both measurements.

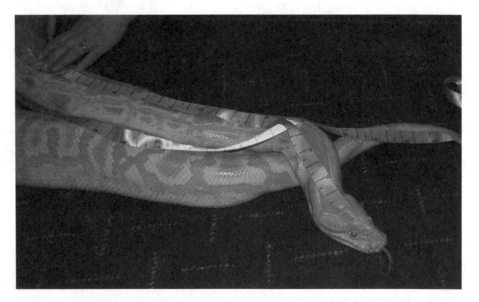

Measuring a 12-foot (3.65-m) albino Burmese python from the middle of its head to the end of its tail.

Philip Blobaum for Iowareptilerescue.com

In a digital twist, a person developed a computer program to measure snakes that works a bit like a dot-to-dot. To use it, you take a digital photograph of a snake next to something with a known length, like a ruler. After you load the photo into the program, you add dots along the snake's back. The program connects the dots to make a virtual string. After you add information about the scale (your ruler), the computer measures the distance between the dots and converts this to match your scale number. Try this on one of your fake snakes at www.serpwidgets.com/main/measure.

and 12 and then look at the picture here. The same 12-inch (30-cm) rubber snake was used for all three pictures. Were you fooled?

The real deal.

Philip Blobaum

Snake on a Stick

Many photos of "giant" snakes show people holding the snake at the end of a long stick. How heavy of a snake could you support?

Materials

Ruler

Pencil

4-foot (1.2-m) broomstick

Handsaw

Net bag (from onions, oranges, etc.)

Cans of food

Masking tape

Adult supervision required.

Use the ruler to mark 25 inches (64 cm), 35 inches (89 cm), and 45 inches (114 cm) from one end of the broomstick. Make a small notch at each mark using the saw.

Put the strap of the net bag at the 25-inch (64-cm) mark. Hold onto the end of the stick and lift the net up to about elbow height. Lower the net and put in one can of food. Lift it again. Keep adding cans until you can no longer hold the net at elbow height. Add up the weight of the cans. Record that number in your journal and on a piece of tape you stick near the notch.

Repeat the same process at the 35-inch (89-cm) and 45-inch (114-cm) marks. What do you notice about your ability to lift weight at a distance? How can this stick be used to weigh things?

Snake scientists often do use a long stick with a hook at the end or a pair of long tongs to pick up potentially dangerous snakes. Photographers have picked up on this and use similar sticks to make a snake look bigger than it is. They put the camera very close to the snake and far away from the person. This creates a false perspective—the person looks smaller and the snake looks bigger.

To make something look smaller, they put it next to an oversized object. The toothbrush used in the photo on page 12 was bigger than a regular one.

OK, so now you want to get up close and personal with snakes. Not so fast—remember, many snakes are becoming rare or endangered. Snake scientists design their studies very carefully and do their best not to harm snakes in any way. They also often have to get special permits. This is because most states and even some countries have enacted laws to protect

How to shoot a snake.

snakes, and rightfully so. Some of the laws don't allow you to even pick up many kinds of wild snakes.

Of course, that doesn't mean you shouldn't look for wild snakes. In fact, even though all the activities in this book are done without a live snake, doing the activities will help sharpen your senses and give you more information about where and when you are most likely to encounter snakes in the wild. Just as ornithologists (bird scientists) have learned a lot about birds by watching them at feeders, you can learn a lot about snakes by observing them from a distance. If you are really interested in handling snakes, it's best to start as a volunteer at a museum, zoo, nature center, or pet store that has snakes. Let the wild ones live their lives naturally, out in the wild, as you increase your snake smarts by doing more activities.

Body Basics

What makes a snake a snake? Snakes belong to a group of animals known as reptiles. Reptiles are animals that:

- have a backbone;

- breathe air using lungs;

- are covered with scales; and

- are **ectothermic** (cold-blooded).

Snakes are different from other reptiles with their strange combination of haves and have-nots. They have skulls, extra jawbones, backbones, scales, and more, but they don't have arms, legs, eyelids, or external ears. Snakes may look like just a head attached to a long tail, but they are very efficiently packaged, highly specialized hunters. The shape of their heads, position of their teeth, bones in their jaws, structure of their skeleton, size and form of their scales, and shape of their tails are all factors that determine their success in where they live and what they eat. Once you get a better understanding of their basic bodies, their actions and reactions will make a lot more sense.

Heads Up!

When I hold a snake for people to touch, most of them will shy away from the head. That's a good thing, because most snakes are pretty nervous when hands loom over their heads. Animals that attack snakes often try to strike the neck right behind the head, so

it's a snake's instinct to jerk around and act defensively. However, a good look at a snake's head provides a lot of clues about a snake's diet and habitat.

The foundation of any head is the skull. Skulls hold all the pieces and parts of the head in place and protect sensitive areas like eyes and brains. Snakes show a lot of variety in the size and shape of their skulls. Puff adders have eyes and nostrils on the tops of their heads so they can watch for prey with the rest of their bodies buried under the sand. Burrowing snakes have stouter bones at the nose to help them push through soil and sand. Vine snakes have thin noses and forward-facing eyes so they have better binocular vision, which makes it easier to catch fast-moving prey. Snakes with large foldable fangs need jaws that open

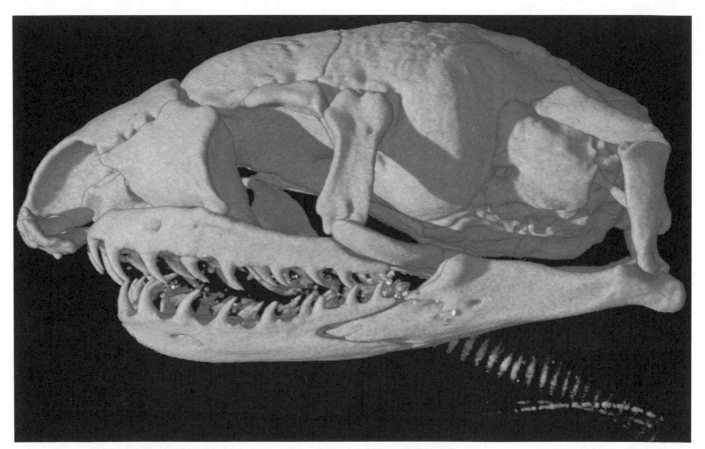

This Calabar ground python has several rows of teeth in the top part of its mouth.

3-D reconstruction based on high-resolution x-ray CT scan courtesy of DigiMorph.org

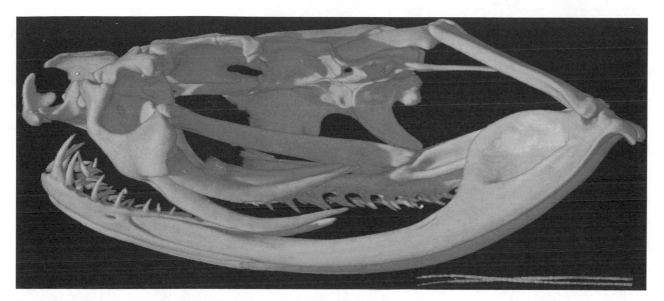

The front fangs fold up and in on this Central American fer-de-lance, which doesn't leave room for additional teeth along the bottom jaws.

3-D reconstruction based on high-resolution x-ray CT scan courtesy of DigiMorph.org

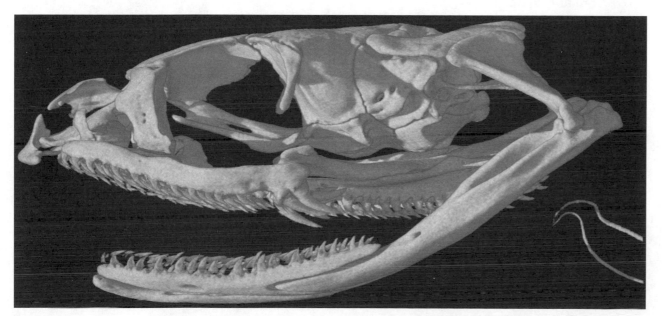

Look at the multiple rear fangs on this striped keelback's skull.

3-D reconstruction based on high-resolution x-ray CT scan courtesy of DigiMorph.org

quite wide. So even if you don't know what type of snake skull you are looking at, a quick glance at its head can give clues about its lifestyle.

Fangs

The most striking feature about a snake's skull is its jaws, the parts that hold the teeth. All snakes have teeth, and the teeth have several jobs. The teeth are very sharp and are curved backward. This shape helps snakes catch an animal, hold onto it so it can't escape, poke it full of tiny holes that help it be digested faster, and pull it toward the throat. To do all this, most snakes have a row of teeth along each lower jawbone (mandible), a row along the top jaws, *plus* two rows of teeth along the middle of the top of their mouths. Boa constrictors often have over 100 teeth!

Of course, the teeth that get the most attention are the fangs. Not all snakes have fangs, and not all fangs are alike. Fangs are longer and thicker than regular teeth because they have the job of delivering venom. Some fangs are like tubes with a hole at the top where the venom goes into the tooth and another hole near the tip where the venom comes out. These hollow tube fangs are found in the front of a snake's mouth. When fangs are in front, there are only two, unless new ones are growing in. Sometimes they are fixed in place, always pointing down. Other times they are foldable, and they rest on the roof of the mouth when not in use.

Snakes that have fangs in the back of their mouths have grooved fangs. These fangs have a narrow groove, like a ditch, running down the front. The venom travels down the grooves into the holes made by the fang tips. Rear fangs fold up like front fangs do, but there can be as many as three fangs on each side of the jaw.

Snake Science

Because a snake uses it teeth like levers to pull food toward its throat, sometimes teeth become stuck in the animal it is eating and get pulled out of the jaw. Luckily, snakes can grow as many new teeth as they need. Sometimes snakes need new teeth every two weeks!

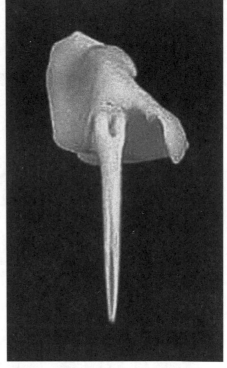

Rattlesnake (tube-style) fang.

Steve Thompson, South Dakota

Fun Fixed and Folding Fangs

A snake's teeth and jaws must work together. Try making a few moving jaws with different types of fangs to examine how snakes' fangs work.

Materials

Pencil

3 cardboard pieces, 8½ by 11 inches (22 by 28 cm) each (Front or back pieces from cereal boxes work well.)

Scissors

Sharp pin

Paper fasteners

Glue

Small rubber bands

Draw side-view outlines of three snakes' heads on the pieces of cardboard. Cut each out so there are three sets with a top skull and bottom jaw (**mandible**).

Use the sharp pin to poke holes through each piece at the back end. Attach a top jaw to a bottom jaw using a paper fastener. Open and shut each set of jaws.

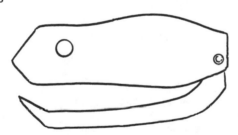

For a fixed-front-fang snake, like a cobra or coral snake, cut out a small cardboard fang from the remaining pieces of cardboard.

Glue it pointing down near the front edge of a top jaw.

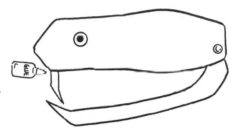

For a foldable-front-fang snake, like a rattlesnake or viper, cut out a long cardboard fang. Use a paper fastener to attach it near the front edge of a top jaw.

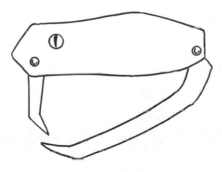

For a foldable-rear-fang snake, like a boomslang or vine snake, cut out two or three medium-sized cardboard fangs. Use one paper fastener to attach all the fangs at one place about two-thirds of the distance from the front of the top jaw.

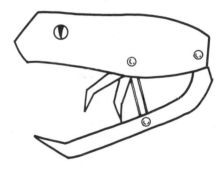

Compare how far each snake has to open its mouth to deliver its venom. What difference do you think that makes? Why?

To make the foldable fangs open automatically, add a paper fastener to the front or middle of the lower jaw, depending on where the moveable fang is located. Put a small rubber band around the back side of the fastener. Holding the cardboard pieces so they don't bend, stretch the band so it goes around the fang. When the jaws are closed, make sure the fang is above the bottom jaw. Hold the top and bottom pieces about halfway back. As you pull them apart, opening the snake's mouth, the rubber band will pull the fang down and into place.

See page 104 for how to make a working fang model!

See page 104 for how to make a working fang model!

Snake Science

Gaboon viper fangs can be between 1.5 and 2 inches (38 and 51 mm) long!

Although snake teeth are very good at doing a lot of different things, they are not made for tearing food into smaller pieces or even for chewing. Some rear-fanged snakes will open and shut their jaws, repeatedly biting an animal to get more venom into it. So it might look like they are chewing, but they aren't mashing their food like you do when you chew. What would your diet be like if you couldn't use your teeth to take a bite out of an apple or chew a piece of bread? You would end up getting your nutrition through liquids like soup and soft foods like applesauce and yogurt.

Snakes, however, are not limited to eating small or soft things.

Strange Snakes

Devon Massyn

Stiletto snakes have the largest snake fangs in proportion to their head size in the world. Also called mole vipers, burrowing asps, and side-stabbing snakes, these snakes have fangs that are so long they point out the sides of their mouths. Instead of opening their mouths and biting down, stiletto snakes just swing their heads around and stab their prey. That's a useful adaptation for a snake that slithers through cramped underground tunnels.

Even without tearing or chewing, snakes can eat animals that are larger and harder than they are

by swallowing their food whole. The secret to this amazing feat is that snakes are missing bones in one place, and have extra ones in another.

Place your fingers directly in front of your earlobes. Open and close your mouth several times to feel how your jaws are hinged together, much like a car door. Snakes' jaws aren't attached to the skull like ours are. Instead, they have an extra bone, called the quadrate, in their jaws. This bone lets their top and bottom jaws separate and stretch farther apart when they are eating.

Next, hold one finger straight up and press it in the middle of your lower lip and your chin to feel where each lower jaw comes together. Snake mandibles aren't fused together like ours are; they are connected by a stretchy ligament instead. This means the sides of the lower jaw can move far apart from each other.

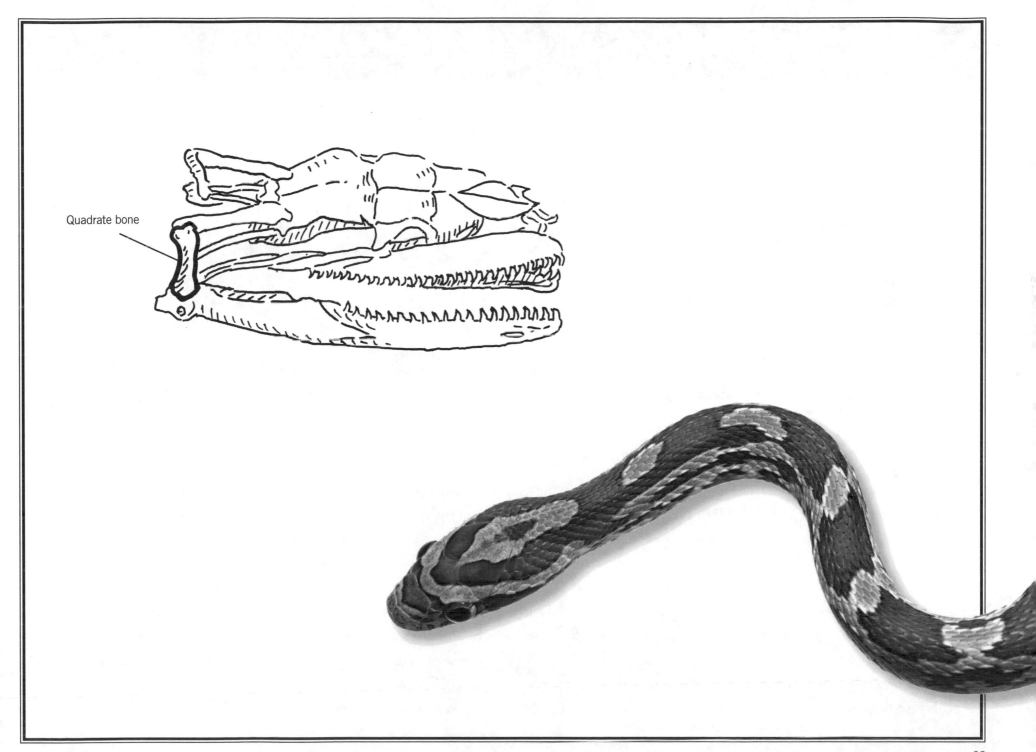

Quadrate bone

The Secret of a Snake's Swallow

What difference do a few bones make? Gather a few materials and find out!

Materials

Friend

Masking tape

Large stuffed animal

2 wide rubber bands

Place the palms of your hands together. Have your friend tape your thumbs together and then tape your little fingers together. Your taped little fingers and thumbs form people-like hinged jaws.

Have your friend tape your remaining three fingers on each hand to each other. This creates attached mandibles.

Pick up a large stuffed animal with your finger-teeth and try to "eat" it, moving the entire animal from your fingertips through your taped jaws and past your wrists—without tearing your jaws apart. Can you do it, or are you going to go hungry?

Remove all the tape except for the piece around the middle fingers on one hand. This will be your upper jaw.

Have your friend hook one wide rubber band over your thumbs and another over your little fingers. You can secure these rubber band "quadrate bones" with small pieces of tape if you want.

Pick up the same stuffed animals with your middle finger-teeth and try to eat it again. You can use those moveable finger teeth on your lower jaw to help you walk

Which fake snake has the jaws that would let it swallow the rabbit?

your top jaws, then your bottom hand jaws, bit by bit over the animal until it all goes down your wrist throat—just like a snake.

A Second Secret

The amazing snake jaws wouldn't make a bit of difference if a snake's skin couldn't stretch around its food as well. Cut off one leg from an old pair of jeans and cut off the toe from a pair of knee-high nylon stockings. Put both arms through the jeans and then make your snake jaws. Can you eat the animal? Try it again with your arms through the stockings to see what a difference stretchy skin makes!

Gape

Even with extra bones, ligament connectors, and stretchy skin, snakes still have muscles and bone sizes that limit how far their mouths will open. An open mouth measurement is called **gape**. A snake's gape depends on how wide its mouth is from side to side, how long it is from front to back, the size of its jawbones, and how its muscles are arranged. There are two different types of gape measurements.

One measurement is the *angle* of a snake's gape. Angles are measured in degrees (°). The very small blind snakes have rigid jaws, much like humans. This means their gape is limited. That's OK, because blind snakes eat mostly ants and termites, so they really don't need jaws that open very wide.

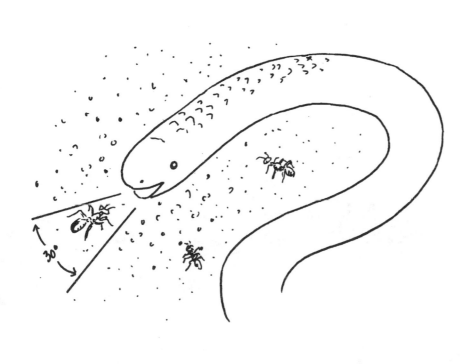

Another snake with a relatively small gape is the rough green snake. It eats mostly insects and spiders. If a snake has a 60° gape, its open mouth would look like the one in the drawing on the right on page 25.

The maximum snake gape recorded is close to 180°—which would look like this photo!

The angle gape measurement can only tell a scientist so much, for a snake with a small mouth but a 180° gape still couldn't eat as much as a snake with a large mouth with just a 90° gape. To better compare snake gapes, scientists created something called a gape index. They measure a snake from the tip of the nose to where the neck starts and record this number. Then they gently press down on the top of the head while it is lying flat on a firm surface. This makes the jaws bulge out a bit on the sides, just like they would while a snake was swallowing something big. The scientists measure from side to side and put the numbers from both measurements into an equation:

$$(\pi \times \text{jaw length} \times \text{jaw width}) \div 4$$

This calculates the gape index. This number helps them compare snakes with different-sized heads.

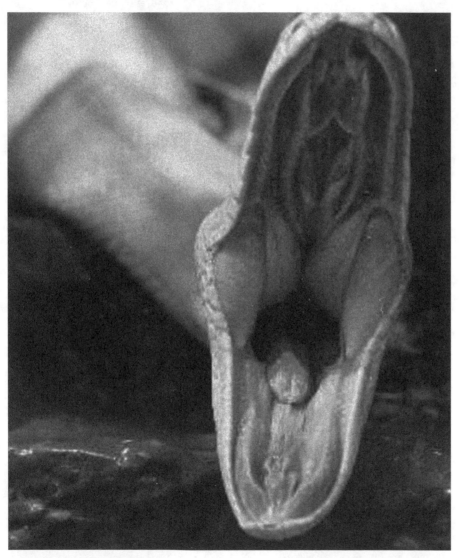

Say AHH!

Big Mouth

A ruler does not provide accurate enough measurements when scientists are calculating gapes. They use an instrument called calipers. You can buy very accurate calipers at woodworking stores, but it's more fun to make your own.

Materials

2 strips of stiff cardboard 12 inches
    (30 cm) long by 1 inch (2.5 cm)
    wide

Scissors

Ruler

Pencil

2 paper clips

Tape

Hole punch

Paper fastener

Calculator

Fold one strip of cardboard in half. Starting about an inch from the end, cut a thin slit out of the middle, leaving a small uncut strip at each end.

Open the strip. Using a ruler, mark a 0 at the far left end, and then mark lines every ⅛ inch (3 mm).

Straighten two paper clips. (Small clips are easier to work with, but larger clips let you measure bigger items.)

Tape one clip to the 0 end of the marked strip so that a long wire hangs down.

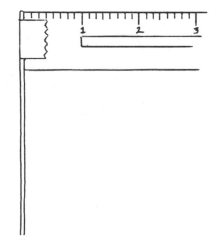

Use a hole punch to make a hole in the second cardboard strip about ⅛ inch (3 mm) from one end.

Tape the second paper clip between the edge and the hole you just made on the second strip. Decorate this second strip.

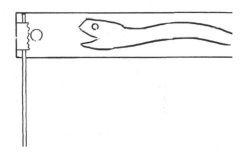

Push a small paper fastener through the hole and then through the middle groove of the first strip. Secure the fastener by spreading the arms. You should be able to slide the top strip along the measuring strip.

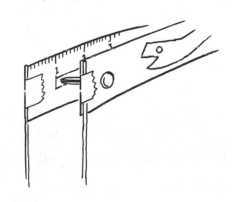

If you are doing this by yourself, it works best if you watch yourself in a mirror to make sure you aren't bending any of the wires. Grin without opening your mouth. Place one wire in the right corner of your smile. Slide the top piece along until the second wire is in the left corner of your grin. Record your jaw width.

Humans don't have long snouts like snakes, wolves, and many other animals, so your next measurement won't be the same jaw length measurement that snake scientists use. Instead, open your mouth as wide as you can, and measure from top to bottom. Record your jaw height.

Put those numbers into the gape index equation, with $\pi = 3.14$.

($\pi \times$ jaw width $\times$ jaw height) $\div$ 4 = _____ your gape index.

Compare your gape index with those of your friends. Who are you going to call Big Mouth?

Be sure to clean the wires between measuring mouths!

Skeleton

Just as the skull protects important parts of a snake's head, the rest of a snake's skeleton, consisting of a backbone and ribs, protects important parts of the body and gives muscles a place to attach so the snake can move. A snake's backbone starts at the back of its skull and runs all the way down to the tip of its tail. In between, there are up to 600 individual back bones, called **vertebrae**.

People usually think of snakes as being incredibly flexible, and they are! But just like you, they can't bend a bone any place except at a joint where the two bones meet. Even then, the ligaments and muscles that connect snake vertebrae to each other, rib bones, and the skin make it so snakes can only bend about 25° between each bone. There are 360° in a circle, so it takes at least 15 snake vertebrae to make a complete loop.

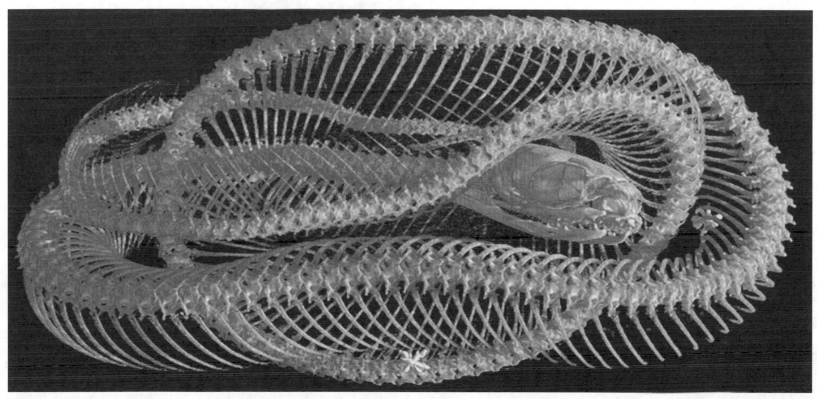

King snake coiled in its egg.

3-D reconstruction based on high-resolution x-ray CT scan courtesy of DigiMorph.org

Make a Snake Spine

Humans have 24 moveable vertebrae, so try this activity with that number of eggs first.

Materials

24 or more 2-part plastic eggs

Drill

String

Needle

Beads, small, medium, and large

Adult supervision required.

Separate the two pieces of each egg. Choose to use either the larger top halves or the smaller bottom halves.

Have an adult drill a small hole in the tip of each egg piece.

Thread the string through the needle and tie a knot.

String your egg halves and beads onto the string to make a snake spine. Alternate egg piece, bead, egg piece, bead, making sure the egg pieces are all facing the same way.

Test to see if the snake can be coiled into a complete circle.

Experiment with the other sizes of egg shells and beads. What is the most flexible snake you can make with the fewest number of pieces?

The shells are tapered, with a narrow end at the bottom and a wide end at the top. This is a bit like snake ball-and-socket vertebrae, which have a ball at the bottom fitting into the slightly larger socket directly under it.

Explore Expanding Ribs

How big of a difference does having free ribs make? Do this experiment to find out.

Materials

Balloon
Cardboard tube
Scissors

Blow into the balloon to stretch it, and then let all the air out.

Put the balloon into the cardboard tube. Inflate the balloon as much as you can.

Remove the balloon and cut a slit halfway up one side of the cardboard tube. This would be similar to a human's rib cage. Put the balloon back in the tube and inflate the balloon as much as you can.

Take the balloon out of the tube again, and cut the slit the remainder of the way up the cardboard tube. This would be similar to a snake's ribs. Replace the balloon in the tube, and inflate the balloon as much as you can.

Record your observations in your journal.

Attached to many of a snake's vertebrae are ribs. In humans, ribs are connected to 12 of the vertebrae close to the head. The very top seven human ribs also connect in the middle at the sternum, creating a protective cage for our heart and lungs, which are very close to each other. Snakes have several hundred ribs connecting to their vertebrae, starting at their neck and running down to the first couple tail vertebrae, but they do not connect in the middle. Unlike people who have arms and legs for movement, snakes need their ribs to help them "walk" across the ground, and connected ribs would limit this movement. A snake's left lung and heart are close to one another, but a snake's right lung is so long that it often stretches clear to its stomach. If a snake had connected ribs for the length of its lungs, its body would not be able to expand as much and it would have to eat smaller prey.

Scales and Skin

Covering a snake's body is its skin. A snake's skin is like yours in that it is breathable, letting air and water in and out, and it is elastic, stretching and growing as a snake eats and grows. It is different in how much it can stretch, how it is shed, and what covers it.

Get a balloon and stretch it without inflating it. This is similar to how much human skin can stretch. Now inflate the balloon about halfway. This is similar to how some snakes can stretch their skin to cover 100 percent more area than normal.

But a snake's skin can't stretch indefinitely. And like human skin, snake skin gets scraped, damaged, too small, and just worn out. In all animals, the older skin separates from the body and dries as new skin is formed. Humans usually shed tiny pieces of skin all the time without even noticing it. Snakes are well known for shedding their skins in one piece. When the old skin is ready to be shed, a snake will rub its nose against something hard to create an opening. Once there is a small hole, the snake will squirm through, leaving an inside-out skin behind.

When you start thinking about snake skin, sooner or later you're going to be wondering about the scales that cover it. Scales are made of keratin, the same thing hair, feathers, and fingernails consist of. Like hair, feathers, and fingernails, each scale is separate, grows directly out of the skin, and is not living tissue. In birds and mammals, most individual hairs or feathers grow long enough that they overlap, creating a layer of protection for the skin, and they can be cut or shed without any pain. In most snakes, each scale overlaps the ones below and beside it too. But in certain snakes, or when a snake is eating a big meal, the skin stretches.

Stretched snake showing skin between the scales.

Andrew M. Snyder

Me too!

Just like your fingernails get larger as you grow, a snake's scales get larger as they grow too.

Super Scales

Create some model scales to test some of the advantages of having scales instead of bare skin.

Materials

1 lb. (0.45 kg) clay

2 to 3 thin plastic lids (from butter tubs or other food containers)

Scissors

Toothpicks

Rock

Separate the clay into two pieces. Mold each piece into a snake the diameter of a toilet paper tube. Try to make them as similar in shape and size as possible.

Cut the thin plastic lids into small, scale-shaped pieces.

Starting at the tail end of one clay snake, press one end of each

plastic scale into the clay, overlapping each piece with the next one until the clay is completely covered. Leave the other clay snake bare.

Imagine the toothpicks were thorns. Test how many places a thorn will stick in each snake. Record your results in your journal.

Test the ability of scales to protect a snake from bumps and bruises by dropping the rock from the same height onto each snake. Record the effect on each model in your journal.

Place both snakes in a place where they will not be disturbed. Check on them once or twice a day until both are completely dry. In your journal, record which one dries out first and how much sooner than the other.

Why do snakes have scales? Scales protect snakes from scrapes, cuts, parasites, and drying out. They are also used for moving. Some scales are smooth, while others are keeled, which means they have a ridge running down the middle. The color and patterns created by scales provide **camouflage** for some snakes and warning coloration for others. The shape of scales on some snakes gives them the ability to make noises that keep **predators** away. Other snakes have some specialized scales that look like horns, eyelashes, or fringed lips.

There are four main types of scales: the head scales; the scales on the back and sides of the body; the long, wide scales, called **scutes**, found on most snakes' bellies; and the scales on the bottom of the tail.

For humans, snake scales offer a way to identify snakes. Sometimes, snakes of the same species can be different colors or their

Parrot snakes have head scales that are easy to see and count.   *Andrew M. Snyder*

color can change as the snakes get older, but from the time it is born, a snake has all the scales it will ever have and those scales are arranged in a predictable way. When scientists are trying to identify an unknown snake, they resort to counting scales. Since there can be thousands of scales on a snake, there are a few tricks or shortcuts they use.

- Head scales on some snakes are big, easy to count, and form an identifiable pattern.
- Snake scientists also take a careful look at the scale that covers the **vent**. The vent is the hole where a snake's poop, babies or eggs, and musk come out. The scale that covers this hole is one

piece in some snakes, or split in two in other snakes.

- Snake scientists have discovered that the number of belly scales a snake has between its head and its vent scale equals the number of vertebrae it has in its body, but not the tail.

Strange Snakes

- Sea snakes' scales lie flat next to each other. This keeps parasites from hiding under their scales, but makes it impossible for sea snakes to move on the land.

- The belly scales on flying snakes are hinged. This helps them flex their bellies inward creating a parachute-like shape so they can glide from tree to tree.

- The scales on blind snakes are the same on the back and on the belly.

Slithering Scutes

Scientists have long known that land snakes move by pushing their bodies off other objects, much like a swimmer pushing off the edge of a pool. They thought that if it was just the muscles doing the work, snakes would be able to move any way they wanted to. But if it was the scales doing the pushing, snakes would only be able to move in certain directions. So which is it?

Materials

Box of spaghetti

Sock

2 colors of 3-inch-square sticky notes

Ruler

Stuff the box of spaghetti into the sock to make a rectangular snake. The sock is the snake skin, and the toe end is the snake's tail.

Fold one sticky note so the bottom edge almost touches the sticky strip. Starting at the "tail" on one broad side, stick the folded sticky note to the sock. The non-sticky fold should face the tail. Keep folding and adding sticky notes as you move toward the head, overlapping the first note by about ¼ inch (1 cm). It should take about 7 sticky notes. Leave a bit of sock closest to the "head" blank to make it easier to pull.

Flip the snake over. This time, fold the other color of sticky notes. When you stick them to the snake, do not overlap them. You will probably use only 3 or 4.

Put your head close to a table and watch the scales as you hold your model by its "lips" and pull it along the table surface. Try pulling it backward. What happens to the scales? Flip it over and watch the scales on the other side as you pull it forward and back. Record your observations in your journal.

Repeat the activity on other surfaces including grass, gravel, shag carpet, and others.

Scales coming off is a bad thing—it would be like pulling out your fingernails! Ouch!

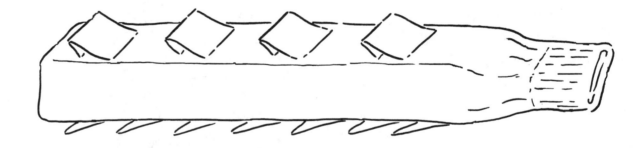

Researcher David Hu and his colleagues performed several experiments to see how scales affect snakes' movements. In one test, they measured the friction of pulling sleeping snakes forward, backward, and sideways across various surfaces. They also covered moving snakes in a special gel so they could photograph where the snakes put most of their pressure as they moved. In their third experiment, they put the snakes in specially made socks and then watched them try to move. Through these experiments, the researchers discovered that without the use of their belly scales, the snakes couldn't move at all. Even with their belly scales, it is very hard for a snake to move sideways and impossible to go backwards.

Interesting Insides

Snakes are more than scales, skin, and bones; they have organs inside their bodies, just like you. They have a heart for pumping blood, lungs for breathing, and a stomach for digesting food. However, to fit everything into a long, slender body, the placement and workings of these internal organs can be a bit different. For example, sea snakes have one lung that stretches almost the entire length of their body. And no snakes pee. Instead, their liquid waste empties into their rectum and exits the body as a white, pasty substance along with snake poop.

What's Inside?

	Organ	What It Does
Digestive System	Esophagus	Tube from mouth to stomach
	Stomach	Digests food
	Liver	Produces bile, which helps a body absorb fats
	Gallbladder	Holds bile between meals
	Pancreas	Produces enzymes that help with digestion
	Intestines	Help with additional digestion and is where nutrients pass through intestine walls into bloodstream
	Rectum	Carries waste away from intestines to exit the body
Respiratory System	Trachea	Breathing tube from mouth to lungs
	Lungs	Special sacs for oxygen and carbon dioxide exchange
Circulatory System	Heart	Muscular organ that pumps blood
	Arteries/Veins	Tubes that carry blood around the body
Excretory System	Kidneys	Control the concentration of chemicals in body fluids
	Fat Bodies	Store solid fats throughout the body

Stuff a Snake

If you were to dissect a real snake, you would discover it has nearly all the same parts that you have. However, some of the parts are relatively larger or stretched longer, and others are smaller. Put together your own snake model to compare and contrast how it all fits together.

Materials

Waxed paper

3 pieces of fruit leather (Fruit Roll-Ups)

Soft candy (taffy, Starburst, Tootsie Rolls, etc.) in four colors

Gummy fruit snacks

Thin licorice strands in the same four colors as the soft candy

Clean scissors

Mini marshmallows

Lay a piece of waxed paper about 20 inches (50 cm) long on top of a table.

Start by making stretchy snake skin. Unroll the 3 fruit leather pieces. Lay them on the waxed paper so they make one long piece with just the edges overlapping. The first two pieces will make up the snake's head and body, while the third piece will become the tail. Press down on the edges so they stick together. You can fold the corners of the top and bottom in toward the middle to make a tapered head and tail.

Pick one color for the snake's digestive system. This system runs from the back of the mouth to the vent and includes the esophagus (the tube that takes food from the mouth to the stomach), stomach,

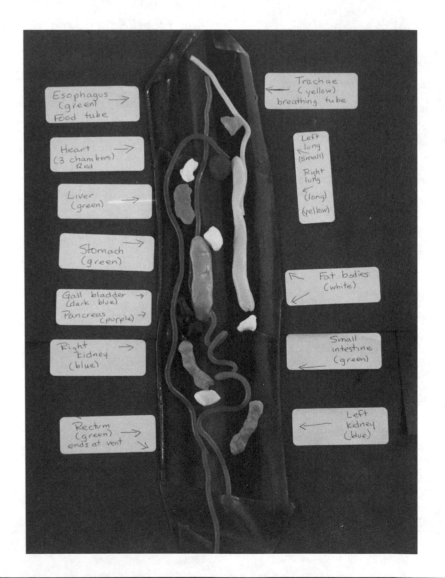

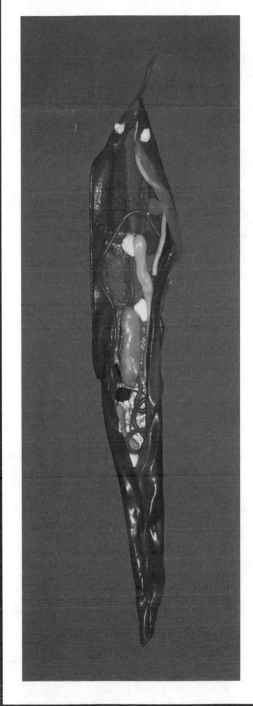

liver, pancreas, gallbladder, intestines, and rectum.

Hold a piece of soft candy in that color in your hand until you can squish it into a long, skinny stomach. Place this piece on the right side in about the middle of the middle piece of fruit leather. Tear a fruit snack of the same color into two pieces (the gallbladder and pancreas) and place them near the bottom left edge of the stomach. These organs produce and hold digestive juices.

Soften another piece of soft candy of the same color to make the liver, but place it a little higher and on the left side of the body, with the bottom edge touching the top edge of the stomach. The liver produces bile to help break down fatty foods.

Cut a piece of licorice in the chosen color to run the length from the front end of one piece of fruit leather to the far end of the second piece of fruit leather (the vent). Lay down the licorice

strip starting about 2 inches (5 cm) from the head end and going under the stomach. After the stomach, make a few bends in the licorice to represent the small intestine (where nutrients are absorbed by the blood) and then position the rest (the rectum, it takes the wastes out of the body) so that it exits the body between the edges of the second and third fruit leather pieces (the vent).

Choose another color to be the respiratory (breathing) system. This system includes the trachea that starts at the tip of the mouth and runs to the lungs. Cut a piece of licorice in the chosen color to run from the tip of the mouth to the top part of the second fruit leather piece. Soften a piece of soft candy and stretch it so it runs from the end of the licorice piece to the top of the stomach. This is the right lung. Cut a fruit snack of the same color into two pieces. Place one piece (the left lung) above and to the right of the right lung. The

small left lung in most snakes is **vestigial**—it is a part of the body that isn't used much, if at all.

Choose a third color to be the circulatory system. Snakes have a three-chambered heart, plus veins and arteries to move the blood around. Place a fruit snack of the appropriate color near the lungs. Add licorice strips of the same color to go up to the head and down to the tip of the tail to represent the arteries and veins.

The fourth color will represent the excretory system. Soften two soft candies in this color. Place one on the right side near the small intestine. Place the other on the left side near the rectum. Make sure both of them touch the rectum at one point, for snakes don't pee. Instead, their liquid waste is passed out along with the solid waste through their rectum.

Place mini marshmallows around the organs to represent fat bodies—the stored fat in your well-fed snake.

Is This the End?

All snakes' bodies end with tails. Even though snakes' tails don't have any internal organs, they are still used in many ways. Cantils use their brightly colored tail as a lure. Puff adders use their tail to bury themselves in the sand. Sharp-tailed snakes have the tip of their spine poking through the end of their tail, which they use to hold onto their slippery prey, slugs. Tree snakes use their tail as an anchor. Yellow-lipped sea kraits, pipe snakes, and Rubber Boas look and act as if their tail were their head, making it harder for predators to know where to strike. Rattlesnakes are well known for their noisy tail tips, and sea snakes have a flattened tail they use like a paddle.

Snake Shapes

Although all snakes have the same basic body parts—skulls, vertebrae, ribs, skin, scales, and tails—each of those parts is a bit different for each kind of snake. When each part is put together, snakes end up being a variety of different lengths and even shapes. Snake cross sections show that a snake's body may be circular, oval, or even triangular in shape. Each shape is suited for a different activity. Burrowing, climbing, swimming, and gliding are four of the actions impacted by shape.

Tree snakes tend to be long and thin, like thick spaghetti. They can move quickly through the treetops, coiling their tail around one branch as an anchor and then stretching across to another branch.

Sidewinders and flying snakes tend to have triangular shapes. This gives them a broad, flat surface to push off the sand or to create a parachute-type arch shape for gliding.

Burrowing snakes are round, which is the best shape for tunneling through soil.

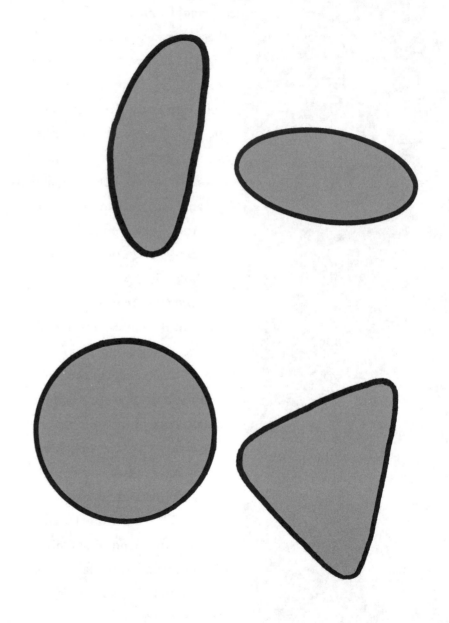

Getting in Shape

For this experiment, pasta noodles make reasonable substitute snakes. Use different types of pasta snakes to do each experiment, and be sure to record your scientific discoveries!

Materials

Pot

Water

Long pasta noodles of various widths
   (lasagna, fettuccini, fusilli, etc.)

Large tub or bucket

Adult supervision required.

Set aside a few pieces of each pasta to use later. Have an adult help you cook the rest of the pasta according to the package directions.

Go outside and test each type of cooked pasta on branches of a tree. Which type of pasta can stretch between branches best without collapsing?

Fill a large tub with water. Pull each type of cooked pasta through the top several inches of water. Which type is the easiest to pull? Which type can move the most water?

Use the uncooked pasta you set aside earlier to test which type can most easily move through loose soil.

3

Awesome Adaptations

Not only do snakes' bodies have some unusual adaptations that help them survive, their body systems work in some unusual ways as well. For example, snakes regulate their temperature by moving to different parts of their habitat. They move by slithering, side-winding, creeping, swimming, climbing, or burrowing. When it gets too cold to move much, they migrate to underground dens. Some snake babies follow scent trails laid down by their mothers to find those dens.

Where did those babies come from? It depends on the snake. Some snakes lay eggs, some snakes bear live babies, some snakes do both, and some snakes do a combination of both. Studying why snakes have these adaptations and how they work offers snake scientists plenty of opportunities to design and do experiments!

Extremely Ectothermic

To stay alive, a snake needs only one-tenth of the energy that a similarly sized mammal would need. This means a snake grows faster when it has food and can go longer between feedings if necessary. Why does it need so little food? It all comes down to how each type of animal uses the energy it gets from food.

The way your body works, it uses much of the energy from the food you eat to shiver, sweat, and do other things to keep your temperature right around 98.6° F (37° C). Instead of using energy from food to maintain one constant body temperature, a snake uses its surroundings to warm up and cool down. This saves food energy for other tasks, but it also means a snake's body temperature can range from just above 40° F (5° C) to almost 100° F (38° C).

You might hear people say that snakes are cold blooded. Scientists don't use that term because it isn't accurate. Sometimes snakes do have cold blood and aren't very active, but other times their blood can be quite warm! The proper term is ectothermic. Ectothermic animals, including snakes, frogs, turtles, salamanders, fish, and others, regulate their internal body temperatures by moving to warmer and cooler places in their surroundings.

Being ectothermic does not mean that being warm isn't important. A snake needs to have a body temperature above 60° F (16° C) to digest food. A snake's body temperature also affects how fast it moves, how often it sheds, how much it grows, how fast injuries heal, and even how snake babies develop.

Snakes will try to maintain a near constant temperature when they can. What is the right temperature for snakes? Most snakes prefer to have body temperatures between 82° and 90° F (28°–32° C). Too hot (above 108° F/42° C) or too cold (32°/0° C) means almost certain death. It's no problem for snakes that live in tropical regions to maintain the preferred temperature—that is the normal air temperature. Snakes that live farther north and south of the equator have to work much harder to warm up and cool down.

Snake Science

If a snake's body temperature falls below 60° F (16° C) while there is food in its stomach, the food will rot instead of being digested. The snake may then die from the poisons rotting food makes.

Basking Basics

If a snake is cold it moves more slowly, making it an easier target for a hungry predator. So a cool snake wants to warm up as quickly as possible. One way to warm up is basking, lying in the sun to absorb its heat. Some snakes have been recorded doubling their body temperatures from around 57° F to 82° F (14° C to 28° C) at a rate of around 2° F (1° C) per minute. Could you find a place to accomplish that?

Materials

Aluminum foil

White paper napkin

Dark paper napkin

Light-colored rock

Dark-colored rock

Flat liquid crystal thermometers

Make a table in your research journal.

Place each item next to one another on an indoor table for 10 minutes. Touch each item and record how it feels to your touch. Use the thermometer to measure the temperature of each item. Record these numbers in your journal.

Place each item outdoors in a sunny area for 10 minutes. Touch each item and record how it feels to your touch. Use the thermometer to measure the temperature of each item and then record it.

Leave the items in the sun for 2 hours. Touch each item and record how it feels to your touch. Use the thermometer to measure the temperature of each item and then record it.

	Temperature after indoors 10 minutes	Temperature after outdoors in sunshine 10 minutes	Temperature after outdoors in sunshine 2 hours	Temperature 10 minutes after removed from sunshine
Aluminum Foil				
White paper napkin				
Dark paper napkin				
Light-colored rock				
Dark-colored rock				

Remove the items from the sun and wait 10 minutes. Touch each item and record how it feels to your touch. Use the thermometer to measure the temperature of each item and then record it.

Is your sense of touch an accurate way to gauge temperatures? Do all the items warm up and cool down at the same rate? If you were a snake, where would be the best place to warm up when the sun is coming up? After the sun has set?

Variations

- Do each test again, but use a spray bottle filled with water to mist each item at the beginning of each trial. What effect does increased humidity have on the warming and cooling rates of each item?

- Place a fan near the items at the beginning of each trial. What effect does wind have on their warming and cooling rates?

For snakes to get to their preferred temperature and stay that temperature, they must move to warmer or cooler places in the habitat. A snake can absorb heat from warm ground, water, air, and sunshine. It can lose heat to cold water, ground, or air, or if its body is in a place with a strong wind. A snake will stretch out to maximize the amount of its body that is exposed, or coil up so only small parts are exposed. A snake that wanted to warm up a lot might stretch out across a black rock in the sun, while one that just needed to speed its digestion might lay with most of its body under a bush, with just the stomach area in the sun. A slightly warm vine snake might dip a few coils off a tree branch to catch a breeze, while an overheated python might go for a swim in the cool waters of a swamp.

Snake Scientist

Scientists studying the ecology of snakes in the field do their best not to disturb snakes any more than necessary. Dr. Charles R. Peterson was studying how fast garter snakes warmed up and cooled down. To determine if what the snakes were experiencing was normal, he needed a control, something that was similar but always changed at a predictable rate. He painted a hollow copper tube with gray auto primer and recorded how fast it warmed up and cooled down, and then compared the results to those of the snakes. His invention is now used by other researchers.

Coiled

S nakes can influence how fast they warm up or cool down by how they place their bodies. How much of an effect does coiling have on heating and cooling?

Materials

2 dish towels of the same color
2 thermometers

Roll each dish towel into a tube shape.

Insert a thermometer in each tube and place the tubes in a sunny area, one tube stretched out, and the other one in a coil. Record the temperature every minute.

Which "snake" warms up faster? How long does it take for both snakes to register the same temperature?

In the sunshine.

In the shade.

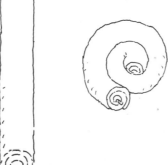

When the two rolls are the same temperature, move them to the shade. Record their temperature every minute. Which one cools faster?

Snake Science

Black rat snakes are so good at soaking up heat from the sun's rays that in parts of the United States, they are one of the first species to emerge from hibernation in the spring.

What About Winter?

There are times when basking on a sunny day just won't warm a snake enough to keep it active. Since the Earth tilts on its axis as it circles the sun, for several months each year one hemisphere is in winter. During the winter when the sun's rays are angled and the nights are long, snakes far from the tropics go into a type of hibernation. The official term for snakes' winter inactivity is **brumation**, but it is similar to the hibernation of some other animals. Many species of snakes gather in large groups in the same place every year. They huddle together as their temperature drops and they breathe less often. Unlike groundhogs, bats, and other furry hibernators, snakes don't sleep all winter, and they don't get skinny. They just slow way down, waiting for it to warm up again. When spring does arrive, having lots of other snakes around makes it easy for males and females to find each other and mate.

Reproduction

While birds, frogs, and turtles lay eggs and mammals have live babies, some snakes lay eggs, some snakes have live babies, some

snakes do either one, and some have eggs in their bodies that hatch right as they are laid (ovoviviparous). There are advantages and disadvantages to each type of reproduction. A female snake that bears live babies often does not eat while pregnant because there is not enough room for both babies and dinner in her body. But she can bask to make sure her developing babies stay warm, and she is constantly protecting her babies from predators. An egg-laying snake will do her best to lay the eggs in a warm, safe place. Grass snakes, milk snakes, and rat snakes have been observed laying their eggs in compost heaps or even piles of manure, where the eggs are likely to stay warm and moist. Mud snakes are known to lay their eggs in the nests of American alligators. Once the eggs are laid, there is not a lot more a female snake can do, so most snake eggs are left unprotected.

Almost 70 percent of snakes lay eggs. Snake eggs are like a combination of hard-shelled bird eggs and slimy frog eggs. Snake egg shells are more like a leather cover than a hard shell. This covering lets air and water in and out while protecting the developing snake from some elements. Snake egg incubation averages around 70 days, although scientists have recorded incubation periods as short as 4 days and as long as 300 days.

Snakes that live where it is cold most of the year have live babies, as eggs would have a hard time staying warm enough to incubate and hatch. Boas, rattlesnakes, and garter snakes also have live babies. In a stranger twist, sea snakes have their live babies underwater, while vine snakes bear their live babies in trees.

Rattlesnake Eggs

In real life, rattlesnakes are ovoviviparous. That means the babies develop inside eggs inside the females. As the female "lays" the eggs, the fully developed baby snakes immediately hatch out and usually stay near their mother for 5 to 10 days. But don't tell anyone that until after they open the envelope!

Materials

Business-size envelope

Pen

Large paper clip

Rubber band

Small paper clip

On the front of the envelope write: Rattlesnake Eggs! Open with care.

RATTLESNAKE EGGS! OPEN WITH CARE

Open the large paper clip so it makes a shallow *U* shape.

Place the rubber band so it is stretched between the two tips of the paper clip. Put the small paper clip in between the two rubber band strands. Twirl the small paper clip until the rubber band looks like a twisted braid. The more you twist it, the longer it will "rattle." Do not let go.

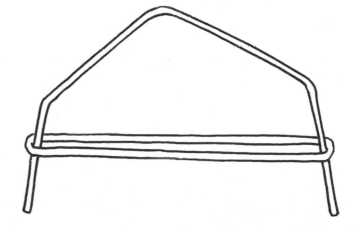

Open the envelope just enough to slip in the wound paper clip with the tips pointed down. Once it is inside, you might want to press down on it with your other hand so that it stays flat.

Close but do not lick and seal the envelope. Put it where a curious person will see it and open it.

When the envelope is opened, the rubber band and paper clip will unwind, making a rattling noise as they hit the paper sides. Act shocked and say, "Wow! I didn't think they'd hatched already!" Then rewind the clip and get ready to trick someone else.

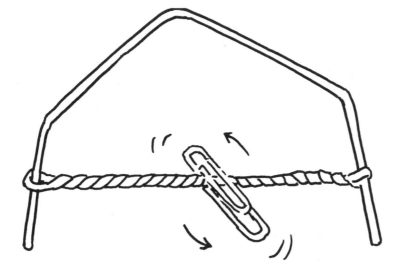

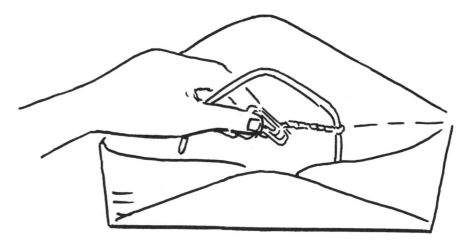

50

Hatch a Tasty Treat

Expect your friends to be surprised at what they find in these sweet treats!

Materials

Flat baking pans

Waxed paper

½ cup butter, softened

1 teaspoon salt

2 teaspoons vanilla

Large mixing bowl

Electric mixer

Large spoon

½ can (7 oz.) sweetened
   condensed milk

5 cups powdered sugar

1 tablespoon brown sugar

24 candy snakes (or worms)

Container with cover

Adult supervision required.

Line the flat baking pans with waxed paper.

Put the butter, salt, and vanilla in a large mixing bowl.

Using the electric mixer, mix the three ingredients until they are fluffy.

Stir in the milk until smooth and then add the powdered sugar.

Use the mixer to beat the mixture until it is a stiff dough. Sprinkle it with brown sugar and then use your hands to knead it until it is smooth.

Curl a candy snake into a ball. Mold a spoonful of the dough in an egg shape around the candy snake. You can also leave one end of the snake poking out of an egg, as if it were hatching.

Place the eggs on the waxed paper–lined pan and let them dry at room temperature for 24 hours. Then store them in a covered container.

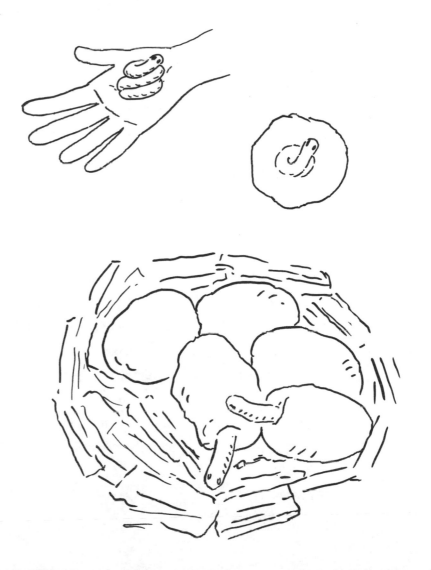

Locomotion

Snakes use their scutes (belly scales) and muscles to move, but that doesn't mean they all move in the same way! Snakes can slither, climb, swim, burrow, side-wind, and even appear to fly. How they move depends a lot on where they are, what is under them, and how fast they want to go.

Most people think of snakes moving in *S*-shaped curves, pushing their bodies against rocks and bumps in the ground, with the body pretty much following the same path as the head. This type of movement is called lateral undulation.

Huge snakes like anacondas, boas, and pythons often appear to move slowly and in a straight line. This type of movement is called rectilinear. Strong muscles pick up some belly scales, move them forward a bit, lift up the belly scales behind them and move them to meet the other ones. A good way to mimic this movement is to pleat the paper wrapper from a straw. Pull the ends apart, release one end, and watch the other one move forward.

To move through narrow spaces or climb trees, most snakes use a concertina- or accordion-type motion. A snake will pull the front third or so of its body up and make bends just behind its head. As it pushes down on the ground with the front part, the tail end of the snake moves forward and into bends, giving the snake leverage to push forward with the front part again. You can see this by pushing and pulling a piece of yarn across a table.

Many different kinds of snakes can side-wind, but the best known one is the sidewinder rattlesnake. Side-winding combines lateral undulation and rectilinear and concertina movements to make a new way to move. To side-wind, a snake must lift part of its body off the ground (similar to concertina movement) as it makes wide bends (similar to lateral undulation) while rolling its body from head to tail (similar to rectilinear motion). This combination of movements makes side-winding snakes appear to almost jump from spot to spot as they move diagonally across the sand.

When a snake is on a smooth surface and is trying to move quickly, you may see a movement called slide-pushing. During slide-pushing, the snake makes irregular bends in its body as it pushes down with parts of its body while lifting up with others. Unlike the other movements, which create somewhat predictable trails, slide-pushing snakes leave an irregular track.

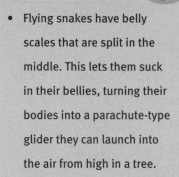

Strange Snakes

- Flying snakes have belly scales that are split in the middle. This lets them suck in their bellies, turning their bodies into a parachute-type glider they can launch into the air from high in a tree.

- Cobras and coachwhips are two of the few snakes that can move in a straight line forward while keeping their upper body raised off the ground.

Lateral undulation

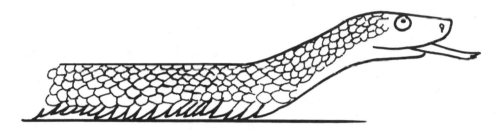

Rectilinear movement

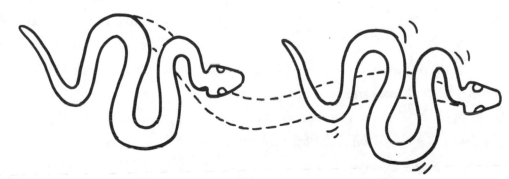

Concertina-type motion

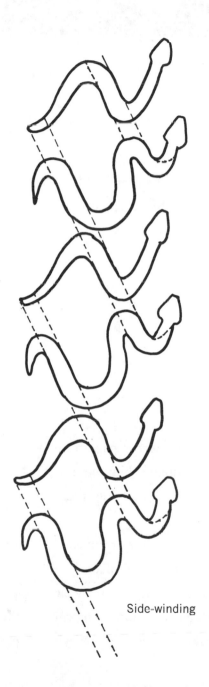

Side-winding

Do the Locomotion

Snakes move so fast it can be hard to see the motions. By creating a flip-book, you can break down the motion into single steps.

Materials

5 sheets of copy paper

Scissors

Pencil

Ruler

Stapler

Cut each sheet of paper into four equal squares. Number the squares 1 to 20 in the lower left corner.

Decide what type of movement your snake will make. The easiest one to draw is usually lateral undulation, followed by concertina and side-winding. Maybe

you want it to start in a coil, move across the page, and recoil.

Start about 2 inches in from the left edge of page one. Use a pencil to draw a snake in its starting

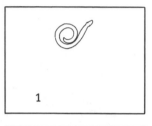

1

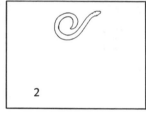

2

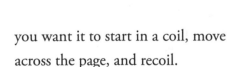

3

position, which could be in a coil, on a tree branch, in an *S*-curve, or however else you want it.

On each of the following pages, draw the snake about ¼ inch

(1 cm) away from the position where it was drawn on the previous page. To create the illusion of motion, alternate the positions of the head, body, and tail. They could be going up, in the middle, and then going down, or in a right curve, straight, and then a left curve.

Stack the papers in order. Staple the left edge.

Hold the stapled edge firmly in your left hand. Hold the right edge in your right hand with your thumb on top. Bend the book and watch the snake appear to move as the pages quickly flip by.

You can also make your snake move backward if you flip from back to front!

Super Senses

Humans learn a lot by seeing, hearing, smelling, tasting, and touching things around them. We use our senses to find our way, locate friends, determine if food is good or bad, get to shelter, keep away from danger, and many other everyday tasks. Snakes have all the same senses to do all the same jobs, but their sense systems work in slightly different ways. One of the best ways to understand snakes is to get inside their senses.

Vision

Most humans use vision more than any other sense to gather information. Most snakes have working eyes as well, but they are not quite the same as humans'. Where they live, what they eat, and when they hunt all influence the type of eyes snakes have.

There are a few things almost all snakes' eyes have in common. Instead of moveable eyelids, snakes have a thin piece of skin, called a spectacle, over their eyes. Most of the time you don't see this skin; however, when a snake is getting ready to shed, a fluid fills the space between the eyes and the skin, making the eyes look cloudy and blue. Of course, the eyes may look blue to us, but other snakes wouldn't notice. Scientists believe that snakes cannot see color. And in almost all snakes, the eyes can't move much to look up, down, to the right, or to the left. They have to turn their heads instead. What difference does this make? Most animals notice things that are moving. If you are trying go unnoticed, you don't want to move your head if you don't have to.

Snake Science

Snakes have only two neck vertebrae. Humans and almost all other mammals have seven neck vertebrae. So not only can snakes not move their eyes very much, they also can't move their neck very far without moving the rest of their body.

Snakes' eyes vary in the shape of the pupils and where the eyes are placed on the head. These are key factors in helping a snake species to survive. Pupil shape affects how much of the world around them a snake can see and how much light is let into the eye. For the most part, snakes that are active during the day have round pupils, which can close to a tiny hole in bright light. Most snakes that are active at night have vertical slits that can open more in the dark, helping them to see better with little light.

The vertical slit pupil on the eye of this Mona boa is almost completely closed.

Jan P. Zegarra/US Fish and Wildlife Service

The round pupil on the eye of this royal green snake is wide open.

Mike Boylan/US Fish and Wildlife Service

See Through a Snake's Eyes

The size of a snake's pupils is controlled by involuntary muscles that react to light. Those muscles can only stretch and contract so far. Make a pair of snake-eye goggles to find out what it's like to see through a snake's eyes.

Materials

2 cardboard tubes of slightly
   different diameters

Scissors

Hole punch

Pipe cleaner

2 balloons

Pencil

2 rubber bands

Cut two 1-inch (2.5-cm) long sections from each tube. Use the hole punch to make a hole in each piece.

Nest each narrower tube inside the larger one, making sure to align the holes. These sturdier tubes will be your lenses.

Connect the two lenses with a short piece of pipe cleaner.

Cut around the outer edge of each deflated balloon so that you have four flat, separate pieces of rubber.

Use a pencil to poke a hole through the center of two balloon pieces. This makes a round pupil. Place one piece over each lens and

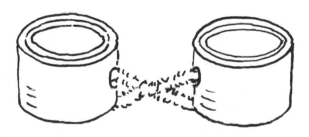

secure them with a rubber band. Look through the lenses.

Remove the balloons and stretch each one as much as possible as you reattach them. How much more can you see with a bigger pupil? Record your observations in your research journal.

Fold the other two balloon pieces in half and cut a small crescent out of the middle of each piece. Place each piece so the crescent is vertically over a lens and secure it with a rubber band. How does this affect your vision?

Remove the balloon lenses and stretch each as much as possible and reattach. Was your field of view larger or smaller than with the round pupils? Turn your lenses sideways to mimic the horizontal pupils of tree snakes.

Record your observations in your research journal.

Test each lens style in dark rooms as well. What other variations in environment can you test? Try them all and record your observations of snake sight!

Field of Vision

Field of vision isn't limited by only the pupil shape; it is also affected by where a snake's eyes are located. Snakes with eyes on the sides of their heads have a large field of vision, allowing them to see more of what is going on all around them, but they have very little visual overlap, which makes it harder to accurately judge distances and speeds. Being able to judge distance and speed is important if you are trying to strike a moving target for lunch! In addition, the snakes that see very little with both eyes at the same time seem to not notice things that are motionless. These snakes are often nocturnal and rely on scent or heat detection to catch their prey.

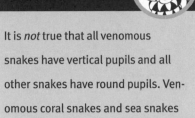
Snakes with eyes near the front of their heads have more visual overlap, which is important for judging speed, distance, and motionless objects, but they have a narrower field of vision. Many snakes that hunt during the day by using sight have forward-facing eyes. Which one works better for you?

The brown tree snake's protruding, forward-facing eyes give it a limited field of vision but good depth perception.

Gordon H. Rodda/US Fish and Wildlife Service

Discover Your Overlapping Vision

The more overlapping vision you have, the better you can judge distance. Snakes with eyes far to the sides of their heads have very little overlapping vision.

Materials

Scissors

3 sheets of copy paper (8.5 by 11 inches)

Tape

Pencil

Tape measure

4 by 6-inch (10 by 15-cm) index card

Baseball cap

Red crayon

Green crayon

Soft ball

Cut each piece of paper into strips 1.5 inches wide and 11 inches long.

Tape the strips together to make one long strip that is 6 feet long (1.8 m).

Fold the paper strip in half so that there are 3 feet (.9 m) on either side. Open it and mark the center line as 0.

Use the tape measure and pencil to mark a line every inch (cm) going both ways from the center. Make sure you write the numbers large enough to be seen from a distance. Tape this strip horizontally on a wall at eye level.

Use tape to attach the index card to the center of the brim of the cap so the card hangs down in line with your nose.

Stand with your back at the 0 mark. Measure a distance of 3 feet (1 m) from the wall and make a tape X on the floor.

Stand on the X and put on your cap. Close your left eye. Looking straight ahead, without moving your head, note the farthest number to the left that you can see with your right eye. Use the red crayon to mark this spot on the strip.

Get back on the X with your cap on. Close your right eye. Without moving your head, note the farthest number to the right that you can see with your left eye. Use the green crayon to mark this spot on the strip.

With the cap on, throw the ball up in the air or against the wall. What do you notice?

The space between the two marks is your overlapping vision.

Take off the cap and repeat the activity to see your true overlapping vision. Repeat the activity with your Snake Eyes in all three variations (round pupils, vertical pupils, horizontal pupils). What do you notice? Record your observations in your journal.

Did you know it's impossible to focus on a near and a far object at the same time? When we want

Snake Science

Snakes with forward-facing eyes have overlapping vision ranging from 30° to 46°. Humans have approximately 120° of overlapping vision.

to look at something far away, the lens of our eyes flattens, making the distance to the back of the eye shorter. For close-up views, our eye lens bulges out, making the eye longer. A snake's lens works in a different way, one that is similar to a camera lens. Instead of changing shape, it moves back and forth—forward to see something close, backward to see something far away.

In Focus

ater is a natural magnifier that is easy to manipulate. Use a sealed bag of water to discover how different eyes focus.

Materials

Clear zippered sandwich bag

Water

Newspaper

Fill the bag about half full with water and zipper it shut. Place the bag on the newspaper.

Test 1. Look directly down at the newspaper print through the middle of bag.

Test 2. Look at the print through the bag near an edge.

Test 3. Hold the bag flat at the edges and lift it about 2 inches (5 cm) off the paper. Look down through the middle, and move it up and down.

The lenses in our eyes change shape to focus. The bag lens was flatter in test 1 and more curved when you looked through an edge (test 2). Instead of changing the shape of their eye lenses to focus, snakes' eyes move forward and backward to focus, like lifting and lowering the bag in test 3.

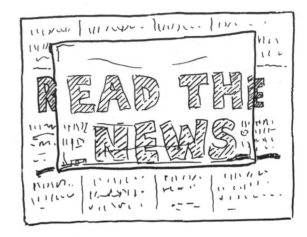

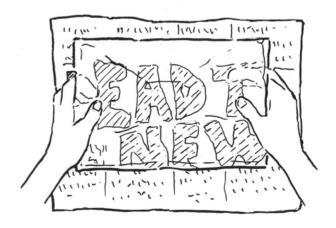

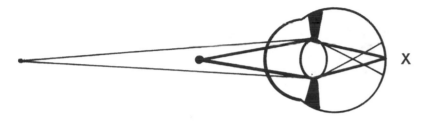

X is where the image is in focus.

Focusing on a near object makes your eye lens bulge.

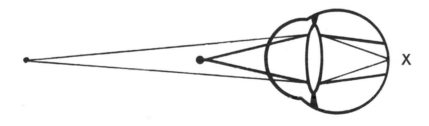

Focusing on a far object makes your eye lens flatten.

Hearing

Humans and many other animals have external ears—holes that start outside our bodies and go inside. We also have pinna, those funny-shaped pieces of skin and cartilage that act as sound catchers on the sides of our heads. Our ears funnel bouncing sound waves down a short tube to three tiny bones that vibrate when hit by the sound waves. The signals these vibrating bones send to our brains are what we think of as hearing.

Snakes don't have any external ear opening, but they do have tiny bones inside their heads. Scientists believe that snakes use vibrations picked up through bones in their lower jaws, other bones, and perhaps even their lungs to make the tiny bones move. If you've ever experienced thunder that makes windows rattle or booming bass music that makes your whole body vibrate, you have an idea of what it's like to feel sounds.

The sound waves made by lower-pitched sounds move better through the ground and a snake's bones than higher-pitched sounds. So snakes can hear the deep tones produced by an approaching car, but they can't hear a high-pitched birdsong. The sounds they sense best are those with the frequency right around middle D on a piano.

Bone Tones

We can hear through bone vibrations too; however, if our ears are working, the airborne sounds overwhelm the bone tones. This project will help you block out airborne sounds to hear like a snake.

Materials

Scissors

String

Ruler

Wire cooling rack

Friend

Wooden spoon

Cut two pieces of string about 12 inches (30 cm) long. Tie one end of each string to the top two corners of the wire rack.

Wind the other end of one string around your index fin-

ger, and then do the same with the other string and other index finger. Press each index finger on the bone behind your ears. Use another finger or your thumb to close your ears.

Have a friend run the wooden spoon gently along the bars of the rack and then gently swing the rack into the edge of a table. Unplug your ears and repeat. What do you notice about the sounds you heard?

Repeat the tests with your string-wrapped fingers held on your lower jawbones. How well can you sense the vibrations now?

Repeat the tests with other metal items hanging from the string, including different sizes of racks, spoons, forks, cans, and kitchen utensils. Can you hear the sounds from bigger ones or smaller ones better?

Me Too!

Some people who are deaf use hearing aids that bring sound waves to the bone just behind the ear.

Smell and Taste

Use your tongue to feel the roof of your mouth, noticing how hard, curved, and bumpy it feels. If you could stick your finger way back (don't try this!), you would find a place where the bone at the roof your mouth (your hard palate) ends. Your soft palate is the skin separating your nose and throat cavities for a short distance, until the two join together near the back of your throat. As you know if you have ever gotten milk up your nose, there isn't much distance between the nose and mouth. Consequently, our senses of smell and taste are closely linked. For a snake, they are even more closely linked.

Snakes have nostrils, just like humans, and these nostrils connect directly to the mouth. Smells, which are chemicals floating around in the air, can drift up a snake's nose, just like they drift up yours. What kind of smells are snakes interested in? They need to know if food, friends, or enemies are nearby and how to find the way home or to a wintering den. But using their nostrils is only one of the ways snakes can make "scents" of what is going on.

You may have heard that snakes "smell with their tongues." This is close, but not exactly true. The job of a snake's forked tongue is to slip through a small hole between the lips, pick up tiny bits of chemicals, and bring them back into the mouth so they can get transferred to the **Jacobson's organ**. The Jacobson's organ is a pair of sacs above the roof of the mouth between the lips and where the nasal tube enters the mouth. Each sac has a separate opening and contains super-sensitive "smelling" cells.

For a long time, scientists thought snakes would flick the two tips of their tongue into the two holes found in the roof of their mouth. But after using special carbon dust and cameras, they discovered that snakes put the chemicals on special pads on the bottom of their mouth. Then those pads are pushed against the two holes, which lead to the Jacobson's organ. The Jacobson's organ is so sensitive that it can determine if more odor particles were picked up by the right or left tip of the tongue! To sense smells even better, some snakes have tongue forks that can spread farther apart than the width of their head. This lets them pick up odors from a wider area.

Garter snakes have distinctive two-color tongues. *Gary M. Stolz/US Fish and Wildlife Service*

Test Your Tongue

Snakes use their nostrils and tongues to sense odors. Can your tongue and nostrils work together to detect menthol, a chemical that acts as a flavor and an odor?

Materials

Pencil

Cough drop with menthol

Crackers

Water

Hard peppermint candy and butterscotch candy

Cinnamon gum and spearmint gum

Strawberries and raspberries

Ground nutmeg and ground paprika

Make a three-column chart in your journal.

One food from each pair listed contains menthol. Can you detect which one?

Start with the cough drop so you can recognize the effects of menthol. Suck on the cough drop for two minutes, trying to keep it far back in your mouth. Record the sensations you notice in your mouth and nose.

Spit out the cough drop. Clean your mouth by eating a cracker, taking a drink of water, and waiting five minutes.

Pick another food from the list to try, following the same procedure as above.

Name of food	My observations	Does it contain menthol?

Snake Science

A snake's sense of smell is not fool-proof. Snakes will strike at nonfood items that smell like prey and ignore prey that doesn't smell right. Scientist Barbara Clucas discovered that young ground squirrels in California chew on shed rattlesnake skins and then lick their bodies to transfer the rattlesnake smell to their fur. Rattlesnakes don't attack the squirrels that smell like rattlesnakes as much as they attack normal-smelling squirrels.

Answers: Peppermint candy, spearmint gum, raspberries, and nutmeg all contain menthol.

Keeping in Touch

Most of the time, you cover a lot of your skin with clothes and shoes to keep you warm, dry, and protected from the sun, scratches, insects, and more. This protection comes at a price—it limits the information you can gather from your sense of touch. The sense of touch is a sense of immediacy. You can smell, hear, or see something in the distance, but you can't feel something from far away. Snakes don't wear clothes. Much of a snake's body is always in touch with the ground, a tree branch, or water, absorbing information about temperature, pressure, texture, humidity, motion, and more.

Exposed!

Find a friend to help you test how you use your sense of touch to learn about your surroundings.

Materials

Swimsuit

Jeans and long-sleeved shirt

Hat, scarf, and gloves or mittens

Socks and shoes

Friend

Completely cover your body with all the clothes listed. Lie on your bedroom floor for 2 minutes. Pay attention to everything you feel—which body parts feel cool or warm, the different textures of various fabrics, and whether some clothes feel tighter than others.

Ask someone to tiptoe and then stomp on the floor around you.

After 2 minutes, strip down until you are only wearing your swimsuit and lie down again.

Once again, keep track of every sensation you experience. Ask your friend to tiptoe and then stomp around you again.

Repeat the activity lying on different surfaces: a hardwood floor, carpet, grass, sidewalk, and so on. What new information about your immediate environment do you gain when less of your body is covered?

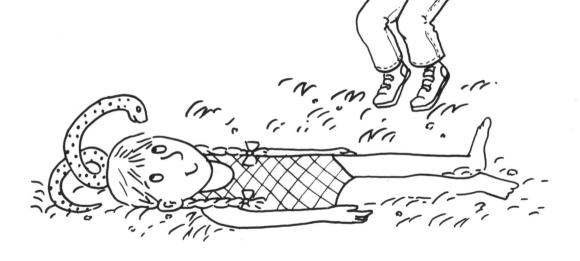

Temperature is basically the amount of heat energy that something has. Since snakes depend on the external environment to adjust their internal temperature, the ability to gauge even slight differences in temperatures can be a matter of life and death.

Heat Seeker

Can you predict which paper snake will be the most sensitive to changes in temperature?

Materials

3 different types of paper (copy paper, tissue paper, paper plate, construction paper, etc.)

Pencil

Scissors

Needle

Thread

Lamp

Adult supervision required.

Draw a coiled snake on a piece of copy paper.

Use a pencil to heavily trace the back side of the pattern. Put this on top of another type of paper. Trace the front side, so the pencil marks will create an exact copy on your other paper. Repeat this for the third paper.

Cut along one line to make a spiral.

Thread a needle with a piece of thin thread and knot the end. Poke the needle through the middle of the snake's head and pull until the knot catches.

Hold a snake spiral above a light bulb of a lamp that has been turned on for a few minutes. Rising warm air will cause the snake to spin. Which snake spins the fastest? Record your observations in your journal.

Take your snake spirals outside on a calm, sunny day. Test them over sunny and shady areas including sidewalks, driveways, gardens, rocks, and grass. Which spiral is the most sensitive?

Nerve endings in your skin are what give your brain information about what you feel. Snakes' skin has plenty of nerve endings, and they are very responsive to being touched. There are some places in nearly all snakes where the scale covering (cuticle) is thinner. This means the nerve endings are closer to the surface, which makes the snake more sensitive to touch in these areas.

Tickle Test

Try the tickle test and see if you can determine where your skin is thinner and thicker.

Materials

Scissors

Ruler

Thread

Tape

Craft stick

Cut a 2-inch (5-cm) piece of thread and tape it to one end of the craft stick.

Hold the stick so the thread is just touching the palm of one hand. Drag the thread across your hand. Can you feel it?

Move the craft stick so the thread is just touching your lips. Drag the thread across your lips. Can you feel it?

Repeat the test on the heel of your foot, toenail, arm, leg, cheek, head, back of your hand, and your back.

Where are you the most sensitive to touch?

Your lips have the thinnest skin and closest nerve endings, while toenails and the soles of your feet are pretty thick.

Be sure to record your findings in your journal!

You might have noticed that the presence of hair made a difference in how sensitive you were to a moving thread. Instead of hair, most snakes have small bumps, called tubercles, on the scales around their heads. Some snakes have tubercles along their bodies. Scientists think snakes might use these extra-sensitive scales when they are courting. Some males rub their chins over the heads of females they would like to mate with, while others entangle their entire bodies.

If snakes are so sensitive, how can they glide over jagged rocks and through cacti and brambles without pain? Snakes can get poked, stung, stabbed, and scraped, just like you. However, their long bodies distribute their weight over a greater area. This decreases the amount of pressure they feel at any one place.

Pressure is the amount of force applied to object. The area over

Most snakes are solitary except when they overwinter or are looking for a mate.

Frank Miles/US Fish and Wildlife Service

which a force is applied influences how much you notice the pressure. Air is constantly pushing on all parts of you, but since it is pushing all over your body and not very hard, you don't usually notice it. You do notice pressure when someone steps on your toe, because that person is applying a greater amount of pressure to a much smaller area.

Under Pressure

Why does it hurt more to step on one rock than to walk or crawl across a gravel driveway?

Materials

Drill

2 wooden 2 by 4-inch boards between 6 and 8 inches (15 and 20 cm) long

Hammer

20–30 nails

2 long balloons

Adult supervision required.

Have an adult drill 8 to 10 rows of three holes ½ inch (1 cm) apart on one board. Hammer a nail through one hole.

Inflate a long balloon and tie it shut. Put it on top of the nail and press down with the second board. How long before it pops? Record your observations in your journal.

Hammer one nail through each remaining hole on the board, making sure they are all exactly the same height.

Inflate a long balloon. Carefully center it on top of the nail points on the board. Align the second board so it is directly over the balloon and board. Watch the balloon as you press down (apply pressure) as evenly as possible. What happens when you apply pressure over a greater area? Record your observations in your journal.

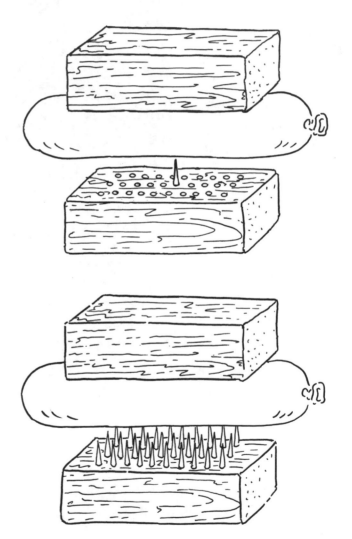

5

On the Offense

Have you ever noticed that snakes don't seem to move much? Whether in the wild or in an exhibit, snakes spend most of their time just lying around, saving their energy for when they need it. When do they need it the most? When they are hungry!

Almost all snakes have to catch moving food to eat; they can't slither up to a plant and take a bite. A few snakes, like those that eat eggs, ants, and baby animals still in their nests, can go to where the food sits still.

Most other snakes find a trail or spot where there is a lot of animal activity and wait to ambush animals that come close. A few snakes actually chase the animals they want to eat. No matter where their food is, to improve their rate of success, snakes use sneaky tricks, super-sensitive cells, poison plays, quick strikes, and super-tight squeezes. Much of the time, their prey never sees them coming.

Lures

Walking along a trail, you spy what looks like a yellow caterpillar next to some plants. Look twice before you reach for it, or you might get a sharp surprise! Cantils, young copperheads, Death adders, and Puerto Rican racers have brightly colored tails that they use as lures to trick other animals like lizards, frogs, and birds. A snake with a tail lure will sniff out a well-used animal trail, curl up with its tail placed in sight and its head hidden not too far away, and then wait, and wait, and wait, for a curious critter to come along. A bird swooping down on what it thinks is a tasty caterpillar will come close, then snatch! The camouflaged snake strikes first.

This young copperhead uses its bright tail as a lure.

Pete Pattavina/US Fish and Wildlife Service

Come and Get It!

Since your sense of smell isn't nearly as good as a snake's, it's easier to create a place where you know animals will come than it is to find an animal trail.

Materials

Shallow dishes

Water

Sunflower seeds

Markers or paint

Shoestring

Set one shallow dish of water and one dish of sunflower seeds on the ground near some cover (bushes, fencing, brush, or an extra-large box) big enough for you to hide behind. Fill the food and water dishes every day until you notice that small animals like birds, mice, lizards, or shrews have found it. Watch for a few days, noting when you see the most animal activity.

While you are waiting, use the markers or paint to turn a shoestring into a camouflaged snake with a brightly colored tail.

On the test day, lay the snake on the ground so the colorful tail is close to the feeding area and can be easily seen, and then hide behind the cover holding the other end. It may take a few minutes before animals approach the area. When an animal looks at the lure or tries to grab it, slowly pull it toward you. How close will the animal get to you? Does it try to eat your lure?

Super Sensitivity

Nearly all animals have temperature-sensitive cells on their skin. Temperature-sensitive cells are the ones that tell you to move your hand away from a hot stove or that your toe is dipped in ice-cold water. In most animals, these cells are widely scattered all over the body. Humans have a couple heat sensitive-cells per square inch of skin.

Temperature sensitivity is even more important to snakes. Since they can't create their own body heat, snakes need the ability to sense differences in temperatures so they can move to the right place to warm up or cool down. Most snakes sense the differences in temperatures through their skin.

There are also super-sensitive snakes. Boas, pythons, rattlesnakes, water moccasins, and copperheads all have exceptionally sensitive heat-detecting pits on their heads. At first, some people thought these holes were ears or maybe extra nostrils. But these holes don't pick up sound waves or smells; they detect heat! To see them, look for small pits along the lips of boas and pythons or right next to the nostrils of rattlesnakes, copperheads, and water moccasins. (It's best if you look at a picture, not a real snake!) In each

of these pits, there are hundreds of thousands of heat-sensitive cells. There are more cells in a snake's pit the size of this *O* than there are on your entire body!

If an object, any object, is warmer than the air around it, it reflects some of that heat as infrared waves. The heat-sensing

cells in the pits detect those infrared waves. Snakes' brains are programmed to use this information to create infrared pictures of the world. The images could be something as solid as a warm rock to lie on or something as soft as a rabbit for dinner.

76

The heat pit on this copperhead is just between the nostril and the eye.

US Fish and Wildlife Service

NASA/IPAC

An infrared rabbit would be easy to see at night!

Courtesy NASA/JPL-Caltech

Hot Lips

As is true for boas and pythons, one of the most sensitive areas on your body is around your lips. Try these experiments to find out what your heat sensitivity is.

Materials

Large metal paper clip

10 cups

Water of various temperatures

Thermometer

Open the paper clip into a *U* shape with the tips almost touching. Press the tips just above your lips. If it feels like a single tip, move the tips out slightly and try again, until you can feel two points. Keep the points at this distance.

Fill 10 cups with different temperature water, from ice water to very hot tap water.

Put one tip of the clip into the hottest water, the other tip into the coldest. Hold the tips in the cups for at least 60 seconds. Pull out the tips and immediately

press them above your lips. Can you tell which point was hot and which was cold? If you could, put the tips in cups that are closer in temperature and try again.

Keep testing your sensitivity until you cannot tell the difference in temperature between the two points.

Use the thermometer to measure the temperature in each cup that last held a paper clip tip. Subtract the smaller number from the larger number to determine your sensitivity level. Record this number in your journal.

Repeat the experiment on different parts of your body. Is the area around your lips really the most temperature-sensitive area you can find?

Saving Snakes

When some snake owners no longer want their snakes, they release them into the wild. This is not good for the snakes or for the native wildlife. There is a big problem in Florida where people have released of a large number of Burmese pythons. See how a herpetologist uses scientist T. H. Bullock's research on heat-sensitive pits to capture these invaders using warm water balloons by viewing the video at http://video.pbs.org/video/1409336716/.

Keeping Food Close

Finding food is only one part of snake offense. Snakes use several methods to make sure their food doesn't get too far away from their mouths. Some snakes grab and hold on, and other snakes inject venom and let the animal go, knowing that it won't travel far before dying. Find out how each system works.

Constriction

Have you heard of snakes that wrap their prey in strong body coils and give it a big squeeze? From giant anacondas to the much smaller king snakes and racers, there is a large group of snakes called constrictors that squeeze, or **constrict**, other animals. Early European and American explorers told stories about anacondas in which the giant snakes were said to "crush pigs and lambs to a mash or pulp and gulp it down forthwith." These stories were repeated so often that for many years people though these snakes, and all other constrictors, crushed the animals they were squeezing.

Later scientists took a closer look at animals they found in constrictors' stomachs. To their surprise, the animals had very few broken bones. These scientists reasoned that the snakes squeezed an animal until it couldn't breathe anymore and died of suffocation.

Snake Scientist

In 1952, before scientists knew what the pits were for, scientist T. H. Bullock at the University of California covered the eyes of a rattlesnake with adhesive tape so it couldn't see and sprayed a sedative into its mouth to block the sense of smell. He placed the rattlesnake in a small cage and dropped in a mouse. The rattlesnake caught the mouse right away. For the next test, Bullock taped the snake's eyes, sedated its tongue, and taped its pits shut. This time, he placed several mice in the cage with the snake. After a few days, the snake had not found any of the mice. He removed the snake, took the tape off its pits, and held it next to a warm light bulb covered with a cloth. The snake struck the light bulb. Bullock concluded that the pits near the rattlesnake's nose were heat sensitive and used for finding prey.

Prey Puke

How do scientists examine constricted prey? There are three common ways. One is to find a snake that has died shortly after it has eaten so the animal isn't digested. A scientist then dissects the snake and examines what is inside (see the photo in the Introduction on page xi). If the snake is alive, the researcher may take x-rays of the snake's belly. The third way is called palpitation. Basically, a scientist gently squeezes a snake, moving from the ventral scale up toward the mouth. By using just the right amount of force, the prey is pushed back up the digestive tube and out the mouth—all slimy and everything. There even have been a few times where an animal was swallowed alive and was "rescued" in this manner!

More recently, herpetologists have taken yet another look at constrictors. They watched and timed how long it took for a constricted animal to die. Their studies showed the animals died before they had time to suffocate. The current theory is that the coils of constrictors squeeze the blood

vessels so blood can't move, and sometimes cause the chest cavity to collapse, stopping the heart from beating. The lack of blood flow to the brain causes death faster than a lack of breathing.

Snake Science

A python can squeeze the life out of a goat or wild pig in less than a minute.

Snake Strength

Constrictors, whether they are giant like an anaconda or smaller like a rat snake, are incredibly strong. See if a shoelace snake you make can squeeze hard enough to stop a fake heart from pumping!

Materials

Bulb baster

Water

Straw

Shoelace

Friend

This experiment is best done outside or over a sink or large pan.

In this experiment, you are using the baster bulb as a heart, the water as blood, the straw as an artery, and the shoelace as a small snake. Fill the baster bulb with water and then put the straw over the tip of the baster. Hold the assembly horizontally and push the baster bulb a few times to get a feel for the amount of effort it takes to push fluid through the artery.

Refill the baster bulb and put the model together again. This time, have a friend wrap the shoelace snake around the straw several times and pull tight. Is your friend strong enough to pull the snake so tight that the blood will stop flowing?

Venom

Almost everything about snakes is fascinating, but one of the most exciting snake characteristics is snake venom! Venom is easy to describe—it's a liquid that a snake injects into an animal to kill it—but scientists are still exploring exactly how it works and why. Each venomous snake species (there are around 250 different kinds in the world) combines different types and amounts of chemicals to make a unique type of venom. All venoms contain chemicals called **enzymes**. Enzymes are proteins that make chemical reactions happen much faster than they normally would.

All scientists agree that once venom gets into an animal, it starts breaking down cells, just like what happens in a stomach. This causes the animal to slow down and often die before the snake can swallow it. But different enzymes work on different cells.

The enzymes in snake venoms affect one of three major systems in an animal's body. Cytotoxic enzymes are a main component in rattlesnake venom. Cytotoxic venoms break down the cells in body tissues, causing heart attacks, creating giant holes at the bite site, or even causing body parts to rot.

Hemotoxic enzymes are found in high concentrations in viper and boomslang venoms. These enzymes affect blood cells, either making blood clot so it can't go through arteries and veins, or preventing blood from clotting, causing bleeding both inside and outside the body. Cobras and Black mambas have venoms with mostly neurotoxic enzymes. Neurotoxic enzymes break down the communication between nerves, causing a body, including the heart and lungs, to become paralyzed.

Not all bites from venomous snakes will kill a person. During some bites, called dry bites, snakes don't inject any venom at all. Other times, snakes might inject only a small amount of venom, which would be painful but not deadly. Some snakes have venom that is only strong enough to kill small prey, not much bigger humans. For bites from highly venomous snakes that have injected a lot of venom, the only real treatment is antivenom.

Antivenom is made by collecting venom from live snakes. To collect the venom, scientists have snakes strike a balloon that is stretched over a collecting glass. Horses or sheep are then injected with small amounts of venom—enough so their bodies make antivenom, but not enough to hurt them. Scientists then remove small amounts of blood from the animals to get the antivenom. The real challenge is to have the right type of antivenom—rattlesnake antivenom won't help someone who has been bitten by a cobra.

Snake Science

Scientists are studying snake venoms to see if they can be used to help humans. A blood pressure medicine has already been developed from the venom of a Brazilian pit viper, and over 60 other treatments have been developed from snake venoms. Scientists are studying other venoms, hoping they can help treat epilepsy, cancer, Alzheimer's disease, and other human diseases and conditions.

Strange Snakes

Nonvenomous king snakes and indigo snakes prey on rattlesnakes; they are immune to the venom.

Virtual Viper Venom

Simulate a cytotoxic snake venom while making a tasty snack using an everyday enzyme.

Materials

Marker

2 clear plastic cups

Fresh or frozen pineapple
    (not canned)

Knife

Measuring cup

2 bowls

3-oz. (90-g) box of red gelatin mix

Spoon

Water

Adult supervision required.

Label one cup *Regular Blood* and the other cup *Viper Bite*.

Have an adult help you cut up fresh or frozen pineapple until

you have about 1 cup (225 g) of pineapple pieces.

Squeeze or mash these pieces in a clean bowl until you have about ¼ cup (60 ml) of pineapple juice. This is your viper venom.

Follow the package directions to make quick set gelatin. Pour half of the warm gelatin into each clear cup.

Add the fresh pineapple juice to the cup marked *Viper Bite* and stir. Set both cups in a safe place to cool. Check on them 30 minutes later. What do you notice?

Imagine the gelatin was your blood. Normally, if you get bitten by an animal so hard that you bleed, your blood thickens, forming a clot so you don't lose too much blood. You can see this in the cup marked *Regular Blood*.

Viper venom has an enzyme that keeps blood from clotting. Not only does an animal bleed from the bite site, as the venom travels through its body, it causes bleeding from the eyes, gums, and internal organs. You can see this in the cup marked *Viper Bite*.

The enzyme in this experiment is a natural product from the pineapple called bromelin. It will *not* cause you to bleed.

Pineapple is heated during the canning process, which destroys the bromelin enzyme that keeps gelatin from gelling.

Further Research

- Make more gelatin, separating it into a number of cups. Add different amounts of the virtual venom to each cup. Figure out the least amount of pineapple juice venom needed to keep the gelatin from gelling. This would be considered a "lethal dose."

- Use a fake fang (page 104) to inject the pineapple juice into the gelatin that gelled. After a while, you should notice that the area around the injection is liquid again. No clotting allowed!

- Just by carefully reading the instructions, can you figure out the antivenom for this experiment? Test your theories before reading the answer at the bottom of the page.

Most Dangerous Snakes

It's hard to pick the most dangerous snake in the world. Is it the snake with the most powerful venom, or the most venom? Should it be the snake that kills the most people because it is common where people live, or the one that kills people the fastest?

- Belcher's sea snake is considered to have the most toxic venom of all snakes.
- The inland taipan (an Australian cobra) is the land snake with the most toxic venom. One bite from this snake could inject enough venom to kill 100 people.
- The saw-scaled viper kills over 20,000 people each year, making it the most deadly snake to humans in the world.
- King cobra venom glands can contain 6 milliliters (1 tablespoon) of venom, enough to kill an Asian elephant or 165 people, and death can occur within minutes.

Snake Science

Snakes do not need to be coiled to strike. They can strike from any position, even underwater!

Snake Strikes

Of course, it doesn't matter how strong one snake is or the power of another's venom if they are too slow in attacking their prey. It's also important for a snake to be able to strike quickly in its own defense if a secretary bird or mongoose is attacking it. Snakes can strike up to half of their body length in about the time it takes you to blink your eyes.

Snake Scientist

Dr. Walker Van Riper of the Denver Museum of Natural History used strobe lights and high-speed photography to time the strike of a rattlesnake. He measured its head moving at about eight feet per second.

Strange Snakes

African water snakes and some litter snakes have tails that will break off if they are pulled by a predator.

Discover Your Striking Speed

Many types of snakes eat lizards. But many lizards have breakaway tails, leaving a predator with just a small bite for its meal. How would you do as a lizard-loving snake lunging at lunch?

Materials

Long pieces of stiff cardboard

Markers

Ruler

Scissors

Friend

Draw three lizards on the cardboard: one 12 inches (30 cm) long, one 8 inches (20 cm) long, and one 6 inches (15 cm) long. Use the ruler to make a line every ½ inch (1 cm), starting at the lizard's head. Cut out each lizard.

Place the side of your forearm on a table with your hand over the edge and your fingers pointed outward like you are ready to pinch something between them. Have your friend hold the large cardboard lizard, head down, directly above your fingers. Without warning, your friend should drop the lizard. Try to close your fingers on it as fast as possible.

Did you get the whole meal or just the tail? Look at the measuring mark and record your results on the back of the lizard.

Repeat the experiment using the 8-inch lizard and then the 6-inch one. Did your times improve? Test your friend's reaction times and then redo the tests using your opposite hand.

6

Definitely Defense

Although snakes are master predators, they are also prey for many other animals, including humans, opossums, hawks, owls, eagles, secretary birds, scorpions, spiders, and even other snakes. What can snakes do to reduce the chances of getting hurt or eaten? Most snakes are not aggressive when they are not hunting and would rather avoid trouble than confront it. For many snakes, the first line of defense is trying not to be seen. If that fails, the next best thing is to escape. The problem with that is snakes really aren't that fast; most snakes slither at a top speed of 3.5 miles per hour (6 km/h). They just look fast because they seem to disappear quickly under leaves, into holes, or even into water. Sometimes, though, a snake may be cornered or the danger may be between the snake and its shelter.

So if a snake is seen and can't escape, what else can it do? Snakes can use some of the same strategies they have for catching prey, like striking and constricting; however, some have additional tricks they can use. Other defensive actions include sound warnings, bluffing, changing colors, emitting a strong-smelling musk, or spitting venom. Which defense would scare you away?

Designer Defense

When you think of a snake, what does it look like? Is it one solid color? Does it have diamonds, rings, or blotches? Is it speckled or striped? Do its back and belly match or are they very different?

Snakes come in many different colors and patterns. Plus, many snakes have patterns that lighten or darken as they age, and there are even a few snakes that can change colors almost instantly! Why is there so much variation?

Each snake has to have the best colors, patterns, and defenses to live as safely and hunt as effectively as possible in its preferred habitat. A water snake hunting frogs in a river should look quite different than a vine snake hunting lizards in a rain forest treetop.

One type of coloration and patterning that is important for many snakes is camouflage. A major element of camouflage is the breaking up of solid shapes and colors. While your home may have one-colored walls and floors, have one-colored walls and floors,

Can you see the copperhead? (Answer on page 107)

CastleLakeEstates.com

most of the time our natural environment does not consist of big chunks of solid colors. A forest floor is littered with leaves, plants, and rotting logs that are dappled with sunlight shining through the canopy overhead. Grasslands are teeming with tunnels through stalks and stems of skinny vegetation. A desert is a mosaic of rocks, sand, shadows, and sunlight. Instead of trying to look like a single leaf, grass stem, or rock, snake patterns take advantage of variations of light and dark.

Scientists group the patterns by their basic forms. They use the descriptions of the colors and patterns as one clue in identifying a snake.

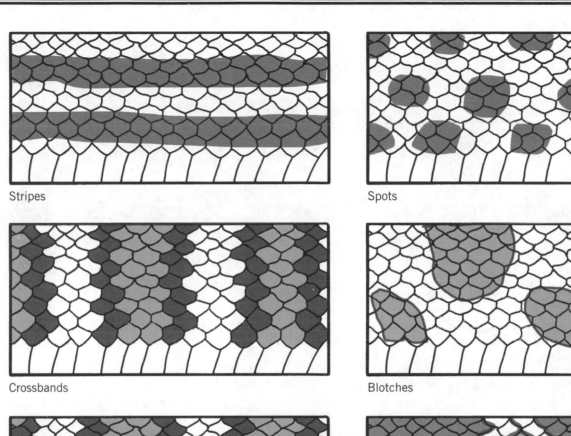
Stripes

Spots

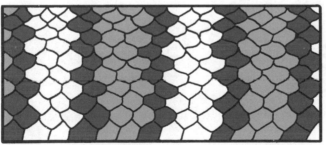
Crossbands

Blotches

Rings

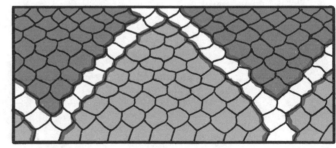
Diamonds

The small plains blackheaded snake's most obvious marking is its black head.

Gary M. Stolz/US Fish and Wildlife Service

The saddled leaf-nosed snake is named for the brown blotches across its back that look like saddles and for its nose shape.

Jeff Servoss/U.S. Fish and Wildlife Service

The night snake has dark blotches on its back and sides.

Gary M. Stolz/US Fish and Wildlife Service

Where Did They Go?

Snakes with patterns suitable for their surroundings can seem to disappear, even if they never move!

Materials

Thin cardboard

Pencil

Scissors

3 crayons (any colors)

Draw and cut out 10 to 12 cardboard snake shapes.

Using the same three crayons, color the back of each snake using a different pattern or color combination.

Take the snakes outside and scatter them in a forested area, a grassland area, a rocky area (gravel driveways are fine), or even on a paved parking lot.

Walk at least 30 steps from the area and look the other way for a minimum of 5 minutes.

When you return, pick up each snake as you see it, recording on the bellies the order in which you found them.

Go to a different habitat and repeat the test.

Does one snake pattern disappear better than the others in all environments?

Repeat the activity using different colored crayons. Is it the patterns or the colors that make the most difference?

Eastern hognose snake.

Ed McCrea/US Fish and Wildlife Service

Snake Science

Scientists can't always rely on colors and patterns to identify snakes. For example, the snakes pictured on this page are both hognose snakes. Hognose snakes (and some other kinds) can be different colors depending on where they live and the color of their parents. Sometimes, to be absolutely sure of a snake's identity, a scientist must count its scales (see page 34).

Western hognose snake.

Gary M. Stolz/US Fish and Wildlife Service

While some snakes use their colors and scale patterns as camouflage, others use them as scare tactics. Many snakes, including water snakes and hognose snakes, spread their head and upper body area so they look bigger (see the western hognose photo on left). Twig snakes and boomslangs add another effect to this defensive posture. Their skin is a different color than their scales, so when they spread their necks they suddenly show a flash of color! How does this burst of color help a snake? A surprise color change can sometimes startle an attacker, giving a snake an extra second or two to slither into a hole, under a rock, or into another safe place.

Presto, Chango!

Make your own color-flashing snake, and practice scaring predators like a boomslang does.

Materials

Balloon

Clothespin

Netting from a mesh bath puff or
    mesh bag of potatoes, onions, or
    oranges

Spray paint

Permanent marker

Adult supervision required.

Fully inflate and then deflate the balloon.

Breathe 1 to 2 puffs into the balloon so that it is slightly inflated. Twist the neck and pinch it shut with a clothespin.

Wrap the netting tightly around the balloon. Spray the balloon with the paint, letting the paint dry before removing the netting or deflating the balloon.

Use the marker to add eyes to the balloon and then deflate it.

Stand in front of a mirror, looking at the "normal" snake. Inflate it as fast as you can, and watch the color change.

Snake Surprise!

American ringneck snakes flip their tails over, flashing the bright red scales on the underside to scare predators away.

As if regular patterns weren't enough, some snakes use patterns to trick other animals! For example, Rubber Boas have very short rounded tails that look a lot like their heads. When a Rubber Boa is threatened, it creates a coil with its head down and its tail sticking up. It will even wag its tail, fooling animals into attacking a nonvital part of its body.

Indian cobras and hognose snakes use a different fake out. Both have dark spots on the backs of their necks. These spots aren't very noticeable until the snake feels threatened. Then it suddenly spreads out its neck and *wow*! The snake has eyes on the back of its head! Most animals would rather ot get face-to-face with a snake, so when they see eyes, they back off. Of course, if they don't back away from a hognose, this snake will roll over on its back, faking its own death.

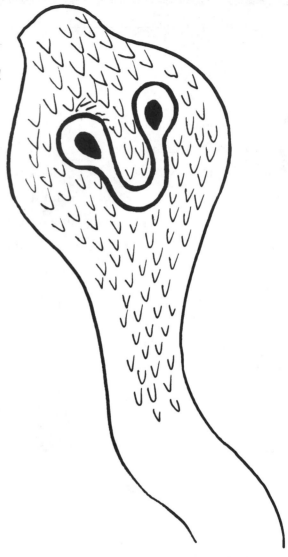

Indian Cobras and hognose snakes fool predators with "eyes" on the back of their head.

Make a Snake Shirt

Like most other animals, snakes notice motion and outlines more than colors. The next time you enjoy the outdoors, sit very still while wearing a snake shirt and see if all kinds of critters come closer to you.

Materials

T-shirt (white, yellow, green, or brown)

2- or 3-gallon pail (a rectangular kitchen garbage can works for larger shirts)

Cardboard

Mesh bath puff

Scissors

Fabric spray paints (whatever colors your desired snake is)

Large disposable cups

Adult supervision required.

This activity is best done outside or in an area with good ventilation. For best results, the project should not be touched or moved until all paint layers are completely dry.

Pull the T-shirt over the pail, tucking the sleeves inside. Hang the bucket upside down or place it on a large piece of cardboard.

Mesh bath puffs are tubes of netting. Cut the string holding the puff together. Open one end of the tube and pull it over the shirt to create a scale pattern. Spray the entire shirt with a light coat of a base color (good colors would be brown, green, tan, or yellow).

Layer the other colors in your desired pattern. Let each coat dry completely before adding another light coat of paint. Do not move the T-shirt or the netting while painting.

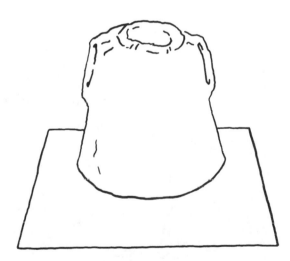

When you are done painting and the paint is dry, remove the T-shirt and the netting.

Pull out the sleeves and place a disposable cup in each one. Wrap netting around the sleeves and paint as before.

When the sleeves are dry, wear the snake shirt with pride!

Optional:

- Use permanent markers to draw an unexpected eye spot in each armpit!
- To make it look like there is a snake on your shirt, start as described above. Use wide tape to create an empty outline of a snake. Cover all the places you don't want painted with paper or tape. Spray as before.

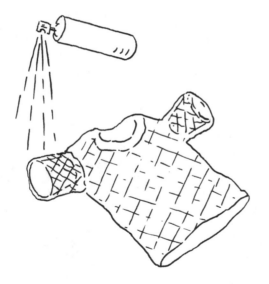

Snake Science

Some nonvenomous milk snakes and Scarlet king snakes have ringed body patterns that make them look a lot like venomous coral snakes. For a long time most people thought the nonvenomous snakes with the copycat pattern were safer from predators. However, not all scientists were convinced, so they did several studies using rubber snake models that had rings or were solid colors. Most often, the ringed snakes were safer during the day but not at night. The confusing part is that coral snakes are most active at night, when their colors wouldn't help them. Does the ringed pattern help coral snakes? Does it help copycats? Can you design the experiment to find out for sure?

What about stripes? Garter snakes and ribbon snakes have stripes running down the length of their bodies, while coral snakes and milk snakes have rings. How do these help the snake hide?

Snakes are striped for several reasons. For example, garter snakes and ribbon snakes often live in open habitats where there aren't areas of dappled sunlight or splotches of shadows. So what we think of as camouflage patterns wouldn't match much of their environment. Long stripes, on the other hand, have at least two functions. The stripes more closely mimic the shapes of grasses and other long-stemmed thin plants. And the stripes mask movement; it is harder to tell where a moving snakes starts and ends when it is striped.

Coral snakes are a completely different story. They have rings that alternate red, yellow, and black—a pattern that is hard to miss. Scientists believe some animals, including coral snakes, monarch butterflies, and even skunks, use bright colors and vivid patterns to warn animals they are poisonous or otherwise a threat. If you can be seen but everyone knows your colors mean trouble, you will avoid getting attacked. So it's defense by design!

A scientist in Borneo picked up a snake that was a reddish brown in color and put it in a bucket. A few minutes later when he got the snake out, it was white. Later on, it was reddish brown again. Why and how do some snakes change color?

Some whys are easier to guess than the hows. Darker skin helps snakes absorb more heat from the sun, warming them up faster. The less time a snake spends basking in the sun, the more time it can be out hunting or hiding in a safer place. And a warmer body leads to faster movement, digestion, and even gestation (development of babies). So it's not too surprising that Hog Island boas are darker during the day and lighter at night, Australian inland taipans become darker during cooler weather, and Madagascan tree boas get darker when they are pregnant.

As for how snakes change colors, researchers are still working to figure that out. However, chameleons, another type of reptile that changes colors, have been studied quite a bit. Chameleons have several layers of cells. Some of these cells are called **melanophores**. The color in the melanophores can be either concentrated in one area or spread throughout the cell. When the color is spread throughout the cell, it covers the colors found in cells below it. Although color changes are a relatively new area of study for snake scientists, some believe that snakes might be changing colors in a similar way.

Make a Color-Changing Snake

You can mimic melanophore mechanisms by weaving a paper snake.

Materials

Construction paper, 2 different colors

Scissors

Ruler

Crayons or markers

Hole punch

Glue

Pick one color of construction paper to be your base color. Cut two strips of this color: one strip 4 inches (10 cm) wide, the other strip 2 inches (5 cm) wide.

Fold each strip in half lengthwise three times. Crease each fold.

Fold the 4-inch (10 cm) wide strip in half width-wise two times. Crease each fold. When it is opened, it should look like a thin checkerboard.

If you put it on a table, it will look like a mountain range. Use scissors to make a small slit at the outer marks on each peak. Flip the paper over and slit the outer marks on the peaks on the back side. These slits will make it easier to cut across later.

On one side of the wide strip, use crayons or markers to color a pattern, making sure it fits within the middle two sections. This forms the snake's body.

Cut a slit across each section, starting and ending at the side slits.

Make the same pattern on each section of the thin strip. This forms the snake's back.

Use the hole punch to make a hole in each section of the back. The small holes will mimic the melanophore cells when the color is concentrated in a small area.

Cut out the pattern in every other section of the back. These larger holes will mimic the mela-

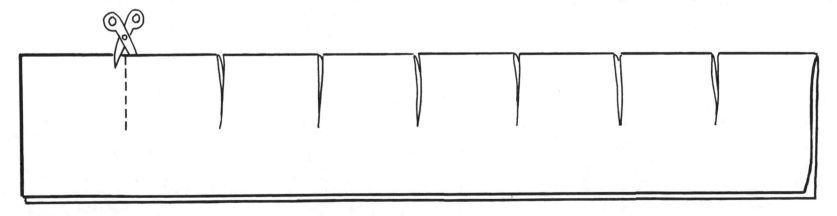

nophore cells when the color is spread over a larger area.

Cut a 2-inch (5 cm) wide strip of the second color of paper.

Glue the two 2-inch (5 cm) strips together.

With the matching color side up, weave the thin strip (over and under) through the slits in the 4-inch (10 cm) strip.

If all your folds are the same size, you should be able to pull the strip so that your snake can appear to change color by simply pulling the center strip forward or back so that one color shows more than another.

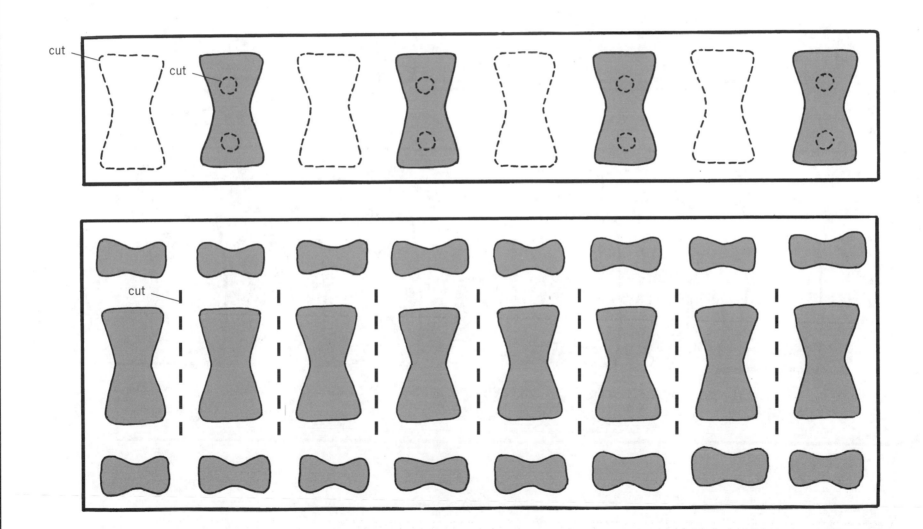

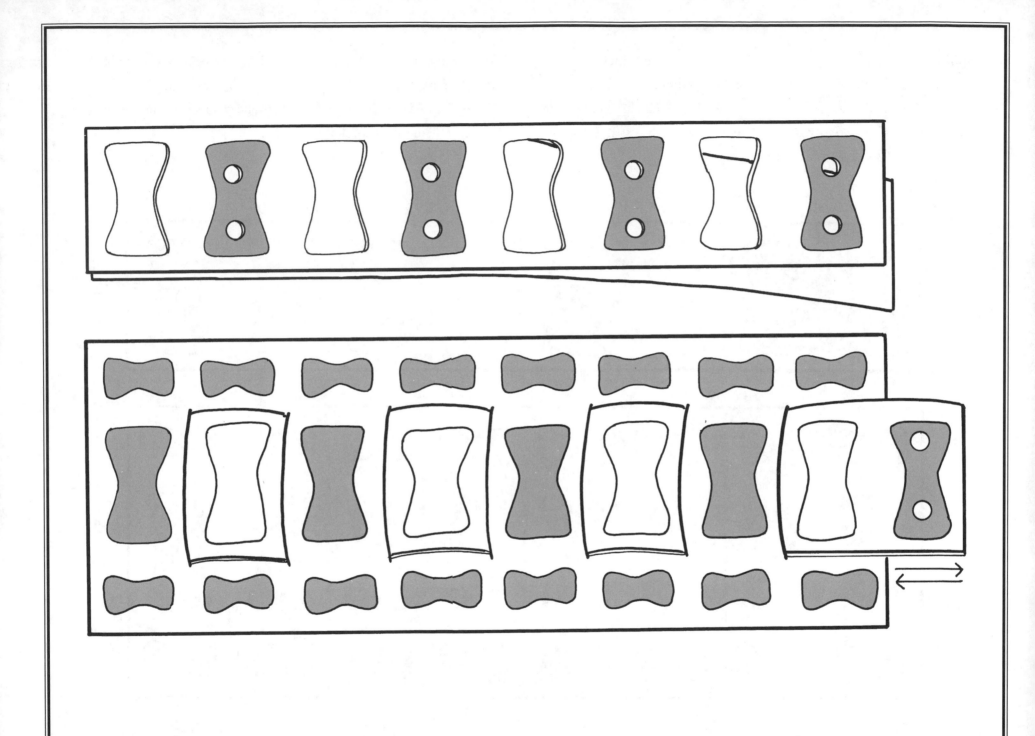

Sounds

Some snakes do such a good job of blending in that they are often in danger of being stepped on. To avoid that possibility, many snakes will make noises to warn animals to keep away. These noises are only made as defensive actions—these snakes would not want to warn their dinner that they are coming. Rattlesnakes are one of the best-known noisemakers, with saw-scaled vipers not far behind.

A rattlesnake's rattle is made of nubs of dried skin, called buttons, that nest on top of one another. A new button is added each time the snake sheds, which happens about four times a year. When the snake shakes its tail, which it can do up to 50 times each second, the skin pieces bump against each other to make a buzzing noise that can sometimes be heard from 60 feet away. Experienced snake scientists can identify the type of rattlesnake

rattling by knowing where each type lives and listening to the sound, because each type of rattlesnake makes a different sound that is determined by its size.

Saw-scaled vipers also make a buzzing sound, but in a very different way. They curl into in a horseshoe shape so the saw-like serrated edges of their scales are touching each other. While curled, they twist and coil, rubbing the scales against each other, making a loud, rasping noise that sounds a lot like a hiss. Since the venom from these snakes is much stronger than the venom of a rattlesnake, this is an important sound to recognize if you are in India.

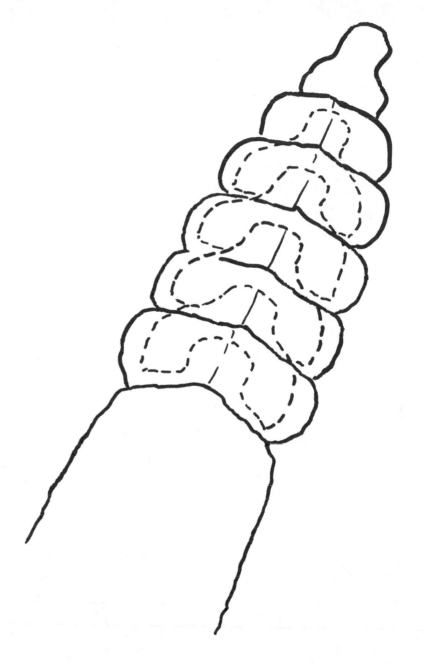

Shake, Rattle, and Go!

From the buzz of a rattlesnake to the bang of a starting pistol, loud sounds are often used as the cue to get moving!

Materials

Pencil

6 3-ounce (89-ml) paper cups

Sock

18-inch (46-cm) piece of string

5 long beads

Use the pencil to poke a hole through the middle of the bottom of each cup and through the middle of the toe end of the sock.

Tie a knot at one end of the string.

Thread the string up through the hole in one cup so the knot is on the outside of the cup. Add a large bead to the thread.

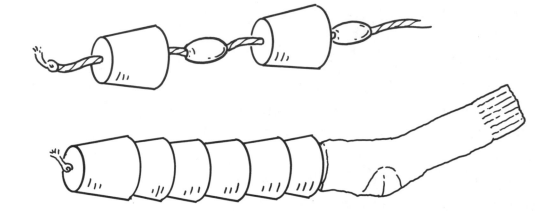

Keep alternating cups and beads.

After threading on the final bead, push the string through the hole in the sock. Tie a knot in the end of the string.

Stick your hand into the sock until it reaches the toe. Hold onto the string and shake your hand as fast as you can. How far away can your rattle be heard?

Spitters

Many venomous snakes have such powerful venom that they can kill animals larger than they ever could eat. So why don't they just bite and kill any animal that is bothering them? Even with a super-fast strike (page 84) and powerful venom (page 82), there's always the danger that the snake will get stepped on, snapped with a beak, or grabbed behind the head. From a snake's perspective, it would be great if they could get their venom into an animal from far away. That is just what certain cobras do. They shoot venom at an attacker's eyes from around six feet (1.8 m) away, a much safer distance than needed for biting.

The truth is, spitting cobras don't actually spit. The holes in the front of their fangs are much smaller than those in other cobras. When they squeeze their venom glands in certain ways, the venom is sprayed out of the holes. In addition, the insides of African spitters' fangs have grooves, which makes the venom spin. Spinning venom has a better chance of hitting its target, just like a football thrown in a spiral pass is more accurate. The target is an animal's eyes. Venom that lands on skin or hair doesn't do much harm, but venom in the eyes causes instant pain, swelling, and temporary blindness. And scientists have recorded that spitting cobras hit their targets between 80 and 100 percent of the time.

Craft a Spitting Cobra Fang

Cobras do not spray their venom at their prey; they spray it when they feel threatened by a potential predator. Create a working model of a spitting fang, using the bulb of a medicine dropper as the venom gland with the tube acting as the fang.

Materials

Saw or pruning shears

Ruler

Wooden skewer

Plastic medicine dropper

Glue

Needle

Match

Water

Animal picture

String

Adult supervision required.

Have an adult use the shears to cut a piece about ⅜ inch (1 cm) long off the tip of the skewer. Drop this into the medicine dropper so that the tip emerges from the end. Secure with a drop of glue.

With help from an adult, heat the tip of the needle using a lit match. Immediately poke the hot tip through one side of the dropper about ¾ inch (2 cm) from the tip.

Fill the bulb with water and then attach your fang. Turn it over and squeeze the bulb.

Use the needle to poke a hole near the top edge in the animal picture and tie one end of a string to it. Tie the other end of the string to a tree branch. Point the bulb at the animal picture and aim for the eyes. How far away can you stand and still hit the eyes 90 percent of the time? How good is your accuracy on a windy day when your target is moving?

Snake Stink

Snakes use their sense of smell to find food, mates, and their winter dens. They can also create their own smells to attract mates, mark territories, and, of course, deter predators. Some snakes use scent glands on their chins and necks, but most of the stronger smells come from paired glands in the tail base that all snakes have.

When certain snakes are picked up, they will open their vent and let loose a nasty smelling combination of poo, musk gland fluids, and sex-related chemical scents, hoping the odor makes the interested animal drop it and run. A cottonmouth will even wave its tail back and forth to spray its musk, which some people says smells like a billy goat, up to three feet (1.05 m) away. What do other snakes smell like? Musk from a European ringed snake supposedly smells like a mixture of mouse manure and garlic, while the smell of rattlesnakes reminds some people of the scent of a wet dog. The fox snake got its common name because the musk it makes smells similar to the musk made by a red fox, which most people think smells like a skunk.

Stink Like a Snake

Can a strong smell really repel a potential predator? Create your own signature stink and test it on animals in your neighborhood.

Materials

Wide-mouth jar with lid

Spoon

Smelly foods (onions, old milk, asparagus)

Small paintbrush

Scout your neighborhood, looking for large rocks, fire hydrants, and sign posts. Monitor these places for a few days, watching to see if dogs stop there consistently to sniff or leave their own scent marks. Pick one of the spots for your test.

Snake musks may be a thick, paste-like substance or a watery, clear liquid. A key ingredient in many smelly animal musks is mercaptan. Look for mercaptan in your kitchen—it can be found in asparagus, onions, garlic, and rotten eggs.

Mix any or all of these ingredients in your jar along with some old, sour milk and other smelly substances. Put the lid on the jar before heading outside.

With the small paintbrush, smear a small spot of your signature smell on your outdoor test location. Keep an eye on the spot for the next several days, and record your observations. Do the dogs act any differently? Are they more attracted to the spot, or do they avoid it? Do they try to rub the scent on their own skin?

106

Strange Snakes

Long-nosed snakes and Caribbean dwarf boas ooze blood from around their eyes, nostrils, and vent when they are frightened.

Keelbacks ooze a nasty-tasling goo from their neck if they are disturbed.

Were you able to find the hidden snake on page 88? The alternating bands on a copperhead's back give it nearly perfect camouflage.

CastleLakeEstates.com

Glossary

Anatomy The body parts of an animal and how these parts are arranged.

Brumation The hibernation-like state of reptiles when they become much less active due to cold conditions. Animals that hibernate are actually asleep, while reptiles that brumate are not asleep; they are just not very active.

Camouflage To disguise things using colors and patterns to hide from enemies.

Constrict To squeeze or press in.

Diameter The distance going straight across a circle.

Ectothermic Controlling your body temperature by moving to warmer or cooler places around you.

Enzyme A chemical that makes certain reactions happen faster.

Gape An open mouth measurement.

Habitat The type of place that is the natural home for a plant or animal.

Herpetology The study of all reptiles and amphibians, a large group of animals that includes turtles, lizards, snakes, tuataras, crocodiles, frogs, toads, salamanders, newts, and efts.

Jacobson's organ The two small sacs located between the roof of a snake's mouth and its nasal passage that are part of the smelling system.

Mandible The bone of the lower jaw.

Melanophore Brown or black color containing cells found in reptiles, amphibians, and fish.

Ophiology The scientific study of snakes, including their anatomy, physiology, behavior, and ecology.

Predator An animal that chases and kills another animal for its food.

Prey An animal that is hunted and eaten by another animal.

Reptile The group of animals that have a backbone, are covered with scales, use lungs to breathe air, and are ectothermic. Reptiles include snakes, turtles, lizards, alligators, crocodiles, and tuataras.

Researcher A person who studies a topic by reading about it, asking questions, and doing experiments.

Scutes The wide belly scales found on most snakes.

Venom A poisonous fluid used by some animals, including snakes, to stun or kill their prey.

Vent The opening on the underside of a snake where eggs, waste, and musk are let out of the body.

Vertebrae Each separate bone found in a spine.

Vestigial A body piece that can no longer work and is not needed.

Resources

There you have it: the basics of snake study. If you have a journal full of notes, pictures, contacts, and questions, you've got the makings of a good scientist. Snake scientists are always coming up with new questions to study and new ideas to try. The resources listed here might just answer some of your questions, or give you new ideas.

General Sources

A good general, secure list of appropriate websites about snakes and other reptiles is available at www.nbii.gov/portal/server.pt /community/reptiles/959.

If you want to know facts about particular snake species, check out *The New Encyclopedia of Snakes* by Chris Mattison (NJ: Princeton University Press, 2007).

One of the best books for directly answering questions about snakes is *The Smithsonian Answer Book: Snakes* by George R. Zug and Carl H. Ernst (Washington, DC: Smithsonian Books, 2004).

If you have a question about snakes and you just can't find the answer, contact the experts by using the Herpetology Hotline, available at http://peabody.yale .edu/collections/vertebrate-zoology/ herpetology/herpetology-hotline.

Chapter Sources

If the activities or information in a certain chapter left you wanting more, use the following resources to further your study of snakes.

Chapter 1: Snake Study
Record Snake Sizes:
- Information about the giant snake fossil along with an artist's rendering of what it might have looked like: http://news.nationalgeographic .com news/2009/02/090204 -biggest-snake-fossil.html
- More information about the endangered Antiguan racer: www.antiguanracer.org/html/ home.htm

Snake on a Stick:
- Photos of supposed giant rattlesnakes and how to tell the stories are exaggerated: http://davidasteen.blogspot .com/2009/07/return-of -giant-killed-rattlesnake.html
- Debunking of a giant snake story: www.foxnews.com/ story/0,2933,497685,00.html

Chapter 2: Body Basics
Heads Up!:
- For more great pictures of snake skulls: http://digimorph .org/listthumbs.phtml?grp=liza rd&name=CommonName
- Watch a stiletto snake side stab its prey at www.youtube.com/ watch?v=4PU53ddi_ww

Super Scales:
- Online/interactive snake identification guide for most North American snakes: www.discoverlife.org/20/ q?guide=Snakes

Interesting Insides:

- See a picture of a dissected snake: http://savalli.us/BIO370/Anatomy/5.SnakeDissection.html

Chapter 3: Awesome Adaptations

Snake Study:

- Learn more about the garter snake wintering dens in Canada: www.naturenorth.com/spring/creature/garter/Narcisse_Snake_Dens.html
- *The Snake Scientist* by Sy Montgomery. Sandpiper Books, 2001.

Do the Locomotion:

- See a digital version of a snake flip-book: www.youtube.com/watch?v=awOo-cMtxr4

Chapter 4: Super Senses

Snake Science:

- Watch a ground squirrel smear its fur with snake skin spit: www.sciencedaily.com/releases/2007/12/071219130305.htm

Under Pressure:

- View the experiment at www.stevespanglerscience.com/experiment/bed-of-nails1

Chapter 5: On the Offense

Venom:

- Watch a snake handler milk the venom from Australian inland taipans: http://vimeo.com/3263747

Striking Speed:

- Check your reaction times online: www.bbc.co.uk/science/humanbody/sleep/sheep/reaction_version5.swf

Snake Science:

- See how strobe light timing works: http://techtv.mit.edu/videos/831-strobe-of-a-falling-ball

Chapter 6: Definitely Defense

Shake, Rattle and Go!:

- Listen to the sounds of various rattlesnakes: www.junglewalk.com/sound/snakes-sounds.htm
- Or hear the sound of a saw-scaled viper: www.youtube.com/watch?v=nfc95jet-dA&feature=related

Snake Speed:

- An easy way to convert your timed run into miles or kilometers per hour is to use this online converter: www.cleavebooks.co.uk/scol/ccspeed.htm

Craft a Spitting Cobra Fang:

- Watch a spitting cobra: www.metacafe.com/watch/39000/spitting_cobra/

Snake Surprise:

- See a hognose snake flash its eyespots and then fake its own death: www.youtube.com/watch?v=COKsb-DZ3zc&feature=related
- Investigate other animals with eyespots: www.environmentalgraffiti.com/animals/news-5-eyespots-frighten

Snake Science:

- Test your ability to identify snakes by colors and patterns: www.ou.edu/oupd/sntest.htm

Teacher's Guide

Kids of all ages are naturally interested in learning about animals. Snake study offers a wonderful opportunity to encourage kids to think beyond fur and feathers and learn about a large group of animals that would greatly benefit from a broader understanding. Some kids may be initially reluctant to learn about snakes, mostly due to unfounded fears caused by lack of exposure or from negative attitudes picked up from media sources or family influence. One of the best ways to address this reluctance is to engage kids with interesting information and hands-on opportunities to make learning personal and relevant. *Awesome Snake Science* is designed to provide these experiences in a nonthreatening format

with the use of activities and models that integrate science, math, and art, creating a framework of knowledge and interest that can support later encounters with live animals.

Most of the activities are open-ended, producing no right or wrong answers but designed to encourage essential skills including questioning, hypothesizing, observing, estimating, recording, and more. These skills form a core of the National Science Education Standards, with specific standards (listed below) that can be met through activities or information presented in the book. Some of the activities will naturally appeal to younger students, while others require skills that are more often found in older students.

The activities that are most easily adapted and explained to students in grades K through 2 are Spot the Snakes, Super Scales, Hatch a Tasty Treat, Bone Tones, Heat Seeker, and Where Did They Go?

Science Standards

Awesome Snake Science was written to encourage kids by posing questions and providing examples of the types of questions and investigations pursued by real scientists in the field.

Unifying Concepts and Processes

Systems, order, and organization

Evidence, models, and
explanation

Change, constancy, and
measurement

Evolution and equilibrium

Form and function

Science as Inquiry

Abilities necessary to do scientific
inquiry

Understanding about scientific
inquiry

Grade Level Standards: Levels K–4

Life Science Standards

Characteristics of organisms

Organisms and environments

History and Nature of Science

Science as a human endeavor

Grade Level Standards: Levels 5–8

Life Science Standards

Structure and function in living systems

Reproduction and heredity

Regulation and behavior

Diversity and adaptations of organisms

History and Nature of Science

Science as a human endeavor

Nature of science

History of science

Although your students can learn a lot about snakes through the use of models and Internet explorations, there is a lot to be said for being able to observe and touch a live snake. If you'd like to offer your students a single encounter with a snake, your best resource may be to contact a local nature center, museum, zoo, or pet store to arrange for a field trip or a classroom visit.

If you want your students to be able to observe and care for a snake for a much longer period of time, be sure to research the laws where you live for information about which snakes, if any, you are allowed to have and if permits are needed to keep them as educational animals. It is relatively easy to keep snakes for observation in the classroom due to their lower energy requirements. However, like all living creatures, snakes require a strong and often long commitment. Once you have a snake as an educational animal in your classroom, you must be committed to caring for it for the duration of its natural life, which can be 10 to 15 years for many species. Most importantly, be sure to secure a captive born snake from a reputable resource—do not try to catch and keep a wild snake. There are a large number of books and Internet resources available on the care and keeping of captive snakes. Consult these before you choose to keep a snake.

If you have access to a live snake for observation and care, the following guides offer additional lessons about snakes and other reptiles and amphibians.

Hands-On Herpetology: Exploring Ecology and Conservation by Rebecca L. Schneider, Marianne E. Krasny, and Stephen J. Morreale, National Science Teacher's Association. Aimed at middle and high school teachers.

What's Slithering Around Your School Grounds by Ms. Terry M. Tomasek and Dr. Catherine E. Matthews. Available at www.uncg.edu/soe/herpetology/herpsweb/Activities.doc.

Pennsylvania Amphibian and Reptiles: A Curriculum Guide Sampler. Available at www.fish.state.pa.us/education/herpsampler.pdf.

Bibliography

Badger, David. *Snakes*. Stillwater, MN: Voyageur Press, 1999.

Balala, Sue. "Enzyme Salad Lab," Access Excellence, accessed July 14, 2010, www.access excellence.org/AE/ATG/data/released/0162-SueBalala/index.php.

Bernard, Robin. *Remarkable Reptiles*. NY: Scholastic Professional Books, 2001.

Boos, Hans E. A. *The Snakes of Trinidad and Tobago*. College Station, TX: Tamu Press, 2001.

Burns, Diane L. *Snakes, Salamanders and Lizards: Take Along Guide*. Minocqua, WI: NorthWord Press, 1995.

Cernak, Linda. *Reptiles A-Z*. Bethesda, MD: Discovery Channel School, 1999.

Christansen, J. L. and R. M. Bailey. *The Snakes of Iowa*. Des Moines, IA: Iowa Department of Natural Resources, 1990.

Conant, Roger. *Peterson Field Guide Series: A Field Guide to Reptiles and Amphibians of Eastern and Central North America*. Boston, MA: Houghton Mifflin, 1975.

Fichter, George S. *Snakes Around the World*. NY: Franklin Watts, 1980.

Gans, Carl (Ed.). *Biology of the Reptilia: Volume 2, Morphology B*. NY: Academic Press, 1970.

Grace, Eric S. *Sierra Club Wildlife Library: Snakes*. San Francisco, CA: Sierra Club Books for Children, 1994.

Greene, Harry W. *Snakes: The Evolution of Mystery in Nature*.

Berkeley, CA: University of California Press, 1997.

Hardy, David L., Sr. "A Re-evaluation of Suffocation as Cause of Death During Constriction by Snakes." *Herpetological Review* 25:2 (1994): 45–47.

"How to Make a Prank Envelope Using Rattlesnake Eggs," WonderHowTo, accessed November 7, 2010, www.wonderhowto.com/how-to-prank-venvelop-rattlesnake-eggs-162752.

Linley, Mike. *The Snake in the Grass: Animal Habitats, Oxford Scientific Films*. Milwaukee, WI: Gareth Stevens Publishing, 1990.

Llewellyn, Claire. *I Didn't Know That Some Snakes Spit Poison: And Other Amazing Facts*

About Snakes. Brookfield, CT: Copper Beach Books, 1997.

LoBue, Vanessa and Judy S. DeLoache. "Detecting the Snake in the Grass: Attention to Fear-Relevant Stimuli by Adults and Young Children." *Psychological Science* 19:3 (2008): 284–289.

Markle, Sandra. *Outside and Inside Snakes*. NY: MacMillan, 1995.

Markle, Sandra. *Snakes: Biggest! Littlest!* Honesdale, PA: Boyds Mills Press, 2005.

Mattison, Chris. *The New Encyclopedia of Snakes*. NJ: Princeton University Press, 2007.

Mattison, Chris. *Snake: The Essential Visual Guide to the World of Snakes*. NY: DK Publishing, 1999.

McClung, Robert. *Snakes: Their Place in the Sun.* NY: Henry Holt, 1991.

Mullin, Stephen J. and Richard A. Seigel (Eds.). *Snakes: Ecology and Conservation.* Ithaca, NY: Comstock Publishing Associates, 2009.

Oldham, Jonathan C., Hobart M. Smith and Sue Ann Miller. *A Laboratory Perspectus of Snake Anatomy.* Champaign, IL: Stipes Publishing Co., 1970.

Oliver, James A. *Snakes in Fact and Fiction.* NY: MacMillan, 1958.

O'Shea, Mark. *Venomous Snakes of the World.* Princeton, NJ: Princeton University Press, 2005.

Parsons, Alexandra. *Eyewitness Juniors: Amazing Snakes.* NY: Alfred Knopf, 1990.

Patent, Dorothy Hinshaw. *Slinky, Scaly, Slithery Snakes.* NY: Walker and Co., 2000.

Peterson, Charles R. "Body Temperature Variation in Free Living Garter Snakes (Thamnophis elegans vagrans)." Thesis, Washington State University, 1982.

Pringle, Laurence. *Snakes! Strange and Wonderful.* Honesdale, PA: Boyds Mills Press, 2004.

Ricciuti, Ed. *The Snake Almanac: A Fully Illustrated Natural History of Snakes Worldwide.* NY: Lyons Press, 2001.

Steen, David. "Return of the Giant Killed Rattlesnake," *Living Alongside Wildlife*, July 21, 2009, accessed October 15, 2010, http://davidasteen .blogspot.com/2009/07/return -of-giant-killed-rattlesnake .html.

Stoops, Erik D. and Annette T. Wright. *Snakes.* NY: Sterling Publishing, 1992.

VanCleave, Janice. *Microscopes and Magnifying Lenses.* NY: John Wiley and Sons, 1993.

"Venomous Sea Snakes Play Heads or Tails with Their Predators," Science Daily, accessed April 19, 2011, www.sciencedaily .com/releases/2009/08/090 805201539.htm.

Zug, George R. and Carl H. Ernst. *Smithsonian Answer Book: Snakes.* Washington: Smithsonian Books, 2004.

Index